Macramé
FOR HOME DÉCOR

Macramé for Home Décor is an original work, first published in 2019 by Fox Chapel Publishing Company, Inc. The patterns contained herein are copyrighted by the author. Readers may make copies of these patterns for personal use. The patterns themselves, however, are not to be duplicated for resale or distribution under any circumstances. Any such copying is a violation of copyright law.

ISBN 978-1-56523-951-7

The Cataloging-in-Publication Data is on file with the Library of Congress.

Photos from *Shutterstock.com*: ivan_kislitsin (2–3); hilalabdullah (4–5 center, 10 bottom right); pronpawit (7); Babich Alexander (8 bottom left); mayu85 (8 bottom right); rawf8 (scissors 9); superelaks (measuring tape 9); design56 (gloves 9); Mega Pixel (masking tape 9); Sinem Babacan (10 top); bogdan ionescu (10 bottom left); iMoved Studio (dowel rod 11); xpixel (tree branch 11); New Africa (bamboo stick 11); chrisbrignell (driftwood 11); yul38885 (bleached driftwood 11); Tanya Sid (paper clips 11); Kathy Burns (crochet hooks 11); and MskPhotoLife (orange thread 11).

Project photography by Mike Mihalo.

Author photo on page 144, © 2015 Daniel Mathieu (*www.DanielMathieuPhoto.com*).

A special thank you to the Poplar Place (@poplar.place.lancaster) for allowing the use of their beautiful home to style all project photography.

To learn more about the other great books from Fox Chapel Publishing, or to find a retailer near you, call toll-free 800-457-9112 or visit us at *www.FoxChapelPublishing.com*.

We are always looking for talented authors. To submit an idea, please send a brief inquiry to acquisitions@foxchapelpublishing.com.

Printed in Singapore
First printing

Macramé
FOR HOME DÉCOR

40 STUNNING PROJECTS FOR STYLISH DECORATING

Samantha Grenier

FOX CHAPEL
PUBLISHING

Contents

Projects

Introduction

Macramé has some extensive ancient roots, but it went into dormancy after a brief craft boom in the 1970s. Sure, sure, there have always been a few knot tyers around, but the general focus turned to knitting and crochet, then onto making cute and kitschy plush toys. Only recently has macramé been creeping back onto the scene.

Fancy materials are not required for macramé. It doesn't need to be expensive either. Cotton is a favorite material of mine and many other knot tyers out there, but it can be pricey. There are alternatives, such as poly blends, hemp, or jute. If the project is not going to bear any weight (such as with a wall hanging), yarns may be used as a substitute. In this book, I list a few alternate materials that can be used project-to-project. The main objective for this book is that something beautiful can be made with materials sourced inexpensively and locally.

NOTE TO BEGINNERS

Tackle any project! Sit down with a couple rolls of cotton crochet yarn and test out each knot. The more you practice, the easier the projects will be.

NOTE ABOUT THE DIFFICULTY LEVEL

I ranked these projects from level 1 to level 3 based on the quantity of knots used and commitment time required to complete. None of the projects in this book are especially difficult to pull off because all the knots practiced on their own are straightforward.

- Knotty Level 1 = Project can be completed in a couple hours (no more than 4) and/or only requires 1 to 2 knots.
- Knotty Level 2 = Project can be completed in an afternoon (4 to 8 hours) and/or requires 2 to 4 or more knots.
- Knotty Level 3 = Project can be completed over a weekend (minimally 12 hours) or longer, and/or requires 3 or more knots.

KNOTTING WITH CORD

I use both universal yarn weights and cord diameters throughout this book. To measure the cord thickness, hold a ruler across the cord to capture the diameter.

When working with longer lengths of cord, form butterfly infinity bundles to prevent tangling. This will also shorten the length of working strands so that you're not endlessly tugging on a piece of string to complete a single knot.

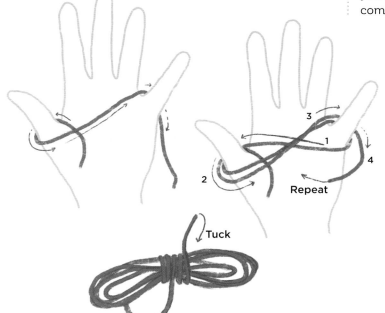

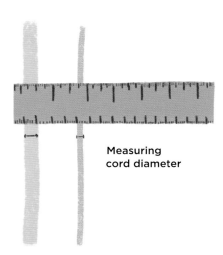

Measuring cord diameter

TENSILE STRENGTH

Tensile strength refers to how much weight a cord can bear before tearing. This is something to keep in mind while making plant hangers and swings. Hangers are typically suspending the weight of whatever it's hanging. When suspending a plant, bear in mind the weight of the potted specimen when it's watered, plus the weight of the pot. As a safety precaution, it is best to keep potted plants under 12" (30.48cm) wide. Suspending the hanger from a stable hook is a must, too. The plant hanger depends on the stability of the ceiling mount just as much as the strength of the cord itself.

Most cords purchased through hobby and craft shops don't offer tensile weight notations, but recommendations are noted for each project in this book. Suggestions are often noted for type of cord (such as acrylic yarn or cotton braid) and either the yarn weight (worsted, bulky, etc.) or thickness measurement. Projects using thinner cords often require a number of strands that will be combined with knotting or braiding to stabilize the finished piece.

Supplies

Working Surfaces and Suspension Options

Project Boards: Typically pre-labeled with measurements, these boards are quite handy. Some are hard and sturdy, some are soft and foamy, while others are self-healing. Project boards are a necessity if your project requires stability. They usually take tape and pins equally well. Sometimes they can be limiting by scale. Often, they are best to use when working on a smaller scale, such as with jewelry projects. The grid and measurements help keep patterns consistent, especially while tying netting and straight rows.

For the projects in this book, I used a large (3' x 3' [1 x 1m]) corkboard purchased from a local craft shop. It doesn't have a preprinted grid, but it is large enough to keep projects neat and stable as I worked.

Foam Core and Cardboard: Need a substitute for to a project board? Foam core and cardboard may be handy. They are not self-healing and may not keep the pins super steady, but measurements can be added by hand and they are often available at a moment's notice. Just be sure when using thinner boards and foam core that you don't pierce the pins straight through the back of your board. That will result in an "ouch!" Pins may not always be necessary, however.

Pillows: Again, these are best used in smaller projects. Pillows don't need to be bulky. I make mine here with just a little batting and foam board. The flat side keeps the board steady while I'm working with the plush side, which acts as cushioning as I work with the foam/flat surface. I simply glued a piece of foam core to a lap desk. Pins won't pierce straight through to the board, but I'm able to tape and pin with a self-drawn grid. While a pillow may not take tape or T-pins so well, it can grip a sinnet strand with safety pins nicely. It beats pinning a project to the pant leg. It's still mobile if you need to travel with your project.

Hooks and Lines: What about large hanging projects? You have a number of options for these if working directly on the floor or table (just don't cut it):

- **S-Hooks:** These can be found in a variety of sizes from a local hardware store, garden center, or plant nursery. S-hooks can be suspended from a hook attached to the ceiling, or suspended from rail, door, or back of a chair.

- **Wreath Hanger:** Readily available around the holiday season, wreath hangers offer a stable hook to suspend a work-in-progress. This is especially handy for tying longer projects, which enable a comfortable seated or standing position.

- **Temporary/Roll-Away Garment Rack:** Coupled with a few S-hooks—or just loosely tied to the bar—a garment rack offers a wide and stable suspension zone for working or storing finished projects. Garment racks of all sorts can be found in the home organization departments of most major retailers.

Essentials

T-Pins: T-pins are recommended companions to work with the project boards because they are not as clunky as thumbtacks or pushpins.

Scissors and Shears: Scissors can be used for every project attempted from this book, but if you plan to use a coarse cord, such as jute or sisal, you may want to use gardening pruners to make cuts to keep from damaging the blades from your favorite trimmers.

Measuring Tape or Ruler: Every project in this book starts with a specific amount of cord. The rulings are shared in both imperial and metric systems. Please choose one and stick with it throughout the pattern.

Tape: In this text we will not be using tape to tack down our projects, so much as using the tape to make cuts to cord ends. This is especially handy for use on twisted materials. It keeps the cord from unraveling while you work. At the end of your completed piece, adding a dab of clear-drying glue will keep the ends tidy and permanent. What type of tape do you need? Any tape you have on hand should work okay, including temporary-hold or washi tape. If you end up cutting the taped bits of your work off, you would be losing maybe up to ¼" (0.61cm), so the stronger the tape, the better.

Glue: One of the best things about needlecrafts is that glue isn't a necessity. Glue is used in this text for the sole purpose of finishing rope ends to prevent them from fraying. Clear-drying fabric glues will have the best hold. If a project (such as a wall hanging) isn't going to be subjected to water, everyday school glues will work just as well.

Extras

Gloves: Working on an extensive project like a large rug can be taxing on your hands. If you work with an especially wiry/hairy/coarsely textured cord, such as jute, working gloves may be flesh saving. No need to rub your skin raw for lovely home decor!

Beads: Macramé beads can be hard to come by. Most are made up of wood, but ceramics can be found if you look closely. The only measure for a bead you need to note is the size of the hole required for threading. Hole sizes of 6 to 10mm on beads are a rare find in jewelry stores, but they can be found. Typically with ceramic and stone style beads, you may need to take to the Internet to find just the right size. Keep in mind that beads are usually measured using metrics, as it's the most universal form of measurement.

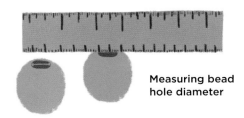

Measuring bead hole diameter

If you find yourself in a pinch for beads, polymer clay and fast-drying clay can be used for making your own. The Internet is loaded with tutorials for making faux-stone beads using just a couple colors of polymer clay. DIY beads offer you the ability to customize the hole size and bead scale all at once. It can be a little extra work, but you would be fashioned with a truly custom and one-of-a-kind project. Same goes for if you find the most perfect bead, just not in the right color. Spray paint comes in a large variety of colors and can also be used against any number of surfaces.

Rings: Rings come in all types of surfaces, from metal to wood. While they can be difficult to come by, stocking up on 1½" to 2½" (3.81 to 6.35cm) sizes are ideal when working with plant hangers. Most plant hanger projects can be modified to skip over the use of a ring (see page 13), but they are quite handy and a quick starting point for such projects. In a pinch, embroidery hoops can be used as substitutes. The wood of embroidery hoops is quite light, so reserve the use of hoops to lighter macramé projects. Hula Hoops® are an excellent option when a larger ring is needed for a project. They're particularly useful when you're creating wall hangings and giant dream catchers (see page 128).

Dowels and Rods: Wooden dowels are readily available at your local hobby, craft, and hardware shop, but mother nature also offers a plethora of twigs, branches, and driftwood that can be used as project supports.

Splicing Tools: Splicing tools can be used to help extend the length of a cord whenever the use of a knot may be too cumbersome. These tools can be difficult to find, so here are a few substitutes:
- Crochet hook
- Beading tool
- Trombone paper clip or piece of floral wire (formed into a hook)

Sewing Supplies: A needle and thread may be more than enough when working with fabric, but sometimes a sewing machine is just faster. A couple projects within this book use strips of fabric to add a little panache to a simple design. When longer strips of fabric are required, baste-stitching the edge of the strips will help prevent excess wear and fray over time. See page 12 for directions on making fabric strips.

Tips and Tricks

Splicing

Sometimes the cord will run a bit short or maybe you would like to extend the size of your project. You can simply tie two pieces of cord together to extend them, discreetly weave a new piece into a knot, or splice the segments into one.

Alternatively, synthetic cords (such as nylon or polypropylene) can be fused together by melting. Remember: *only* use this technique on synthetic cords; this is not suitable for natural fibers, as they will catch fire. Fusing with heat can be fragile, so I do not recommend using this on any weight-bearing projects (such as plant hangers). Hold two pieces parallel and briefly run a heat source (flame of a lighter used here) over the ends (a). Quickly bring the two ends together (b) and allow the melted points to cool completely.

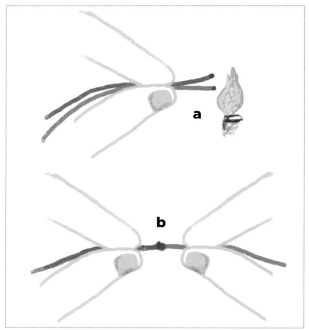

Splicing remnants

Fabric Strips

Fabric is cut and knotted in the projects in this book to add a little more color and pattern to some of the simpler designs. When appropriate, fabric can be cut from scrap or remnant articles into pieces with a width of 1" to 2" (2.54 to 5.08cm), or longer strips from bolt fabric. Here are two ways fabric strips are made in this text:

- **Strips:** Bolt fabric or fat quarters were purchased or found when pieces 2' (60.96cm) or shorter were required. Fabric shears are required for this method. Find the longest edge of the fabric to be used, then fold the fabric horizontally from the shorter edge. Fold to a point which the fabric can still be sheared by scissors, but so few cuts will need to be made. This will keep the edge of the fabric relatively straight. Measure off the desired width and cut one straight line. The resulting fabric ribbons will likely fray, so a fray preventative can be added to the fabric edges and left to dry before handling.

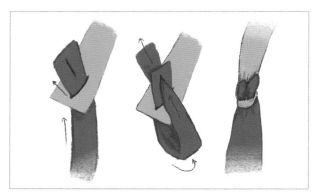

How to add fabric strips

- **Remnants:** Remnant pieces, long or short, can be combined to create a lovely boho-style fabric strip. Either ends can be sewn as shown, or pieces can be spliced together. To splice, cut a small slit into each of the adjoining ends. Feed end A up through end B, then take the opposite end of strip B and feed it up through end A. Gently tug the ends together.

Plant Hanger Loop

The top of a plant hanger requires a loop so it may dangle from a hook. The easiest starting point is to center cords on a metal ring, but a metal ring doesn't always match the plant hanger aesthetic, or one may not be available. Here's the pattern used in this text for starting off a hanger by making a wrapped loop:

In addition to the materials for the plant hanger pattern, cut an extra 6' to 7' (1.83 to 2.13m) piece of cord in the same color, and maybe a small piece of string in contrasting color. Gather and find the center plant hanger cords and tie the contrasting string in the center to mark it. Shift up about 2" (5.08cm), and center the 7' (2.13m) piece of cord from this point (a). Form a series of square knots over the entire bundle of cords (b). The center string can be removed temporarily for knotting; re-tie the string to mark the center again. Once the covered portion reaches 4" (10.16cm) long, fold at the center point (c) and gather all the cords together (d). Continue to square knot around the bundle of cord until the working ends can no longer form knots (about 2" [5.08cm]) (e). The center marker can be removed at this point.

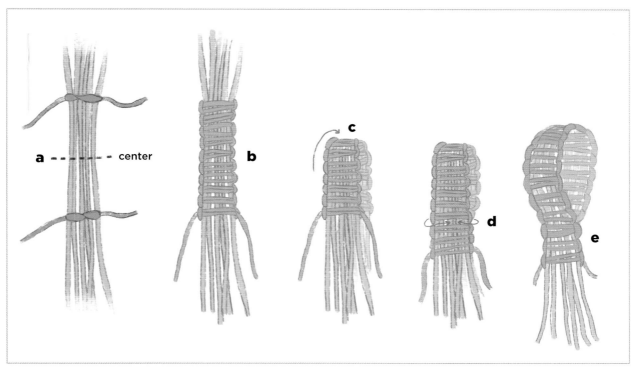

Making a plant hanger loop

Finishing Techniques

Whether the cord is twisted, braided, or knitted, it can come undone. To prevent the cord or yarns from unraveling over time, there are a few ways to combat the unraveling, or just simply work with it.

Bind with glue: Add a dab of clear drying craft or tacky glue to the tips of any cords that can unwind. Best used on natural materials. Just a touch is all that's needed.

Use a finishing knot:
- Overhand knot
- Square knot
- Wraps

Melt it: Only do this with synthetic cords! Natural materials will catch on fire.

Acrylic paint dip: Much like using glue on the tips of the cord, the acrylic paint will bind the ends together, plus add a touch of flair.

Embrace the fray: Unwind the cord as soon as you wrap up the project. Use a macramé brush or basic comb to straighten and fluff.

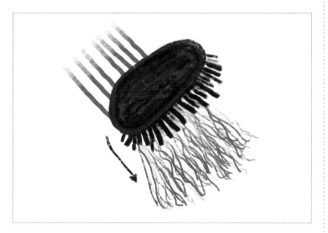

FAUX FEATHERS

Faux feathers can be replicated using just about any twisted fiber. In the examples below, feathers are formed using ordinary crochet cotton yarn.

Left: reef knot; right: half-knot

- **Reef Knot:** One strand is required for mounting, and at least 48 6" (15.24cm) strands are required for the feathering.

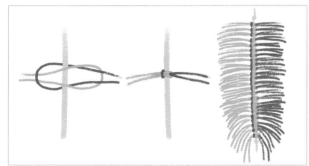

- **Half-Knot:** One strand for mounting, and 48 8" (20.32cm) strands for the feathering. A square knot (page 22) may be ideal to keep the cords secure; however, a half-knot may be sufficient.

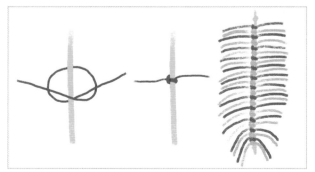

TASSELS

Tassels can be substituted for faux feathers or used as an embellishment on any wall hanging. To make a tassel from yarn, wrap one continuous piece around the width of a hand (or a squat book for longer tassels). Form at least 20 to 24 rotations to make the tassel full; the more rotations, the thicker the tassel will become. Once the optimal thickness is achieved, cut the yarn free. Clip a piece of yarn at least 8" to 10" (20.32 to 25.40cm) long, then thread and center this at the top of the tassel through the gap formed by the fingers. Tie the ends of this yarn together with an overhand knot, then pinch the top of the tassel to prevent it from moving around. Clip another 18" to 24" (45.72 to 60.96cm) piece of yarn, then wrap the top of the tassel. Clip the loops at the bottom of the tassel. The tassel can be trimmed to the desired length, or just to neaten up the ends.

This same technique can be achieved with fabric or ribbon. Fabric strips will fray over time. For fabric strips greater than ¼" (0.64cm), the hanging loops can be first cut vertically to form thinner hanging tassel ribbons.

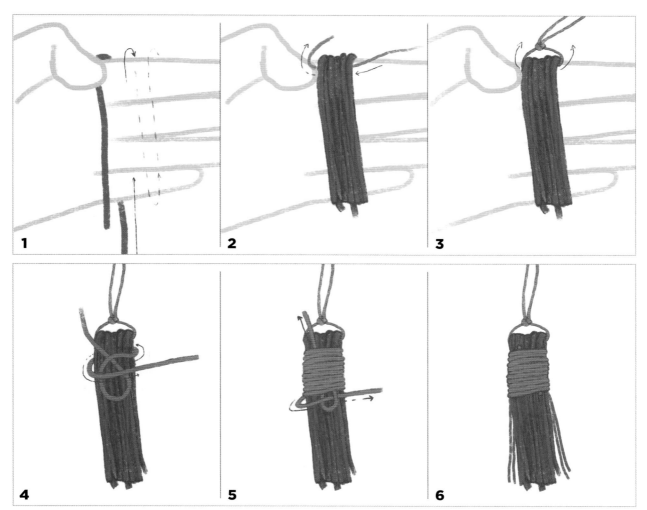

Substitute tassels for faux feathers

Knot Guide

Hitches, Knots, and Braids

Macramé is the decorative art of knot tying. Not all knots are "knots," but all of the tying techniques combined can make some lovely macramé art. A *knot* is defined as cord joining together, whereas a *hitch* is a cord binding to another object (this includes another cord). Another way of thinking of it is that knots are locking to themselves or together, and hitches are grabbing onto something else (or even itself). *Braids* (also known as plaiting) are cords interlocking into a pattern forming a decorative weave.

WORKING STRANDS, CORES, AND ANCHORS

The working strands are the pieces of cord being used to form a knot, hitch, or braid. Sometimes a knot is tied around another strand, or even a bundle of cords; this would be the core. Half-knots and square knots are often tied around other cords to form a core. This helps bulk up the knot for visual effect. An anchor is another cord or object (such as a dowel) the working strand(s) hitches or fastens to. For example, the lark's head knot cords hanging from a dowel are hanging off an anchor.

SINNETS

A sinnet is the repetition of a single knot in a vertical row (column). The most common knot requiring a sinnet is the half-knot. By repeating a half-knot over and over again, it will form a playful spiral.

ALTERNATE PATTERNS

Alternate patterns are how one makes a net. The cords from one row are carried down to a second row, and the working or core strands are paired off with adjacent strands from knots on the previous row.

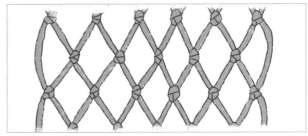

Alternate half-hitch net

Square knot net

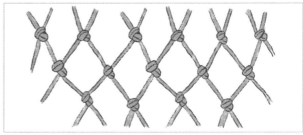

Overhand knot net

HITCHES

Left: lark's head knot; center: reverse lark's head knot; right: double lark's head knot

Lark's Head Knot (LHK): This knot is often used to start a macramé project.

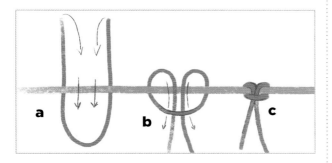

1 Form a loop (often by finding the center of the working cord), and fold or hang the loop behind an anchor (a).

2 Feed the working strands through the center of the loop (b) and tighten (c). This knot is best known for its cartoon frog appearance, when made correctly.

Reverse Lark's Head Knot (RLHK): This is just the backside of a lark's head knot. Some crafters may prefer the aesthetics of this side. It is a bit more minimalist: two dashes with strands hanging in between.

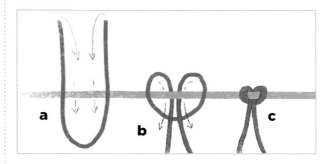

1 To make this, form a loop in front of the anchor (a).

2 Fold the working strands over the anchor, then pass them through the loop (b) and tighten (c).

Double Lark's Head Knot (DLHK): This can also be reversed, if desired.

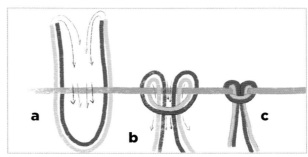

1 To form, find the center of two strands and form a loop (a).

2 Fold the loop over to the backside of an anchor, then feed all the working strands through the loop (b) and tighten (c).

Working Lark's Head Knot (WLHK): This knot is also known as a cow hitch. It is just another lark's head knot formed as a project is underway. It can be used as a substitute for a clove hitch, if preferred.

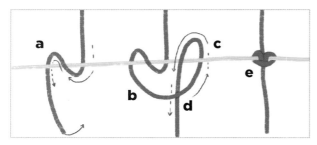

1 To form, draw the working strand over the anchor and loop the strand around the anchor once (a).

2 Draw the working strand across to the other side of the hanging cord (keep the working strand parallel to the anchor) (b).

3 Fold the working strand behind and over the anchor (c), feed the end through the formed loop (d), then tighten (e).

Clove Hitch (CH): This is a great starting and finishing hitch to form fringe.

Left: clove hitch (horizontal); right: clove hitch (vertical)

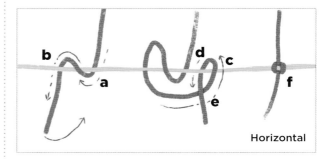

Horizontal

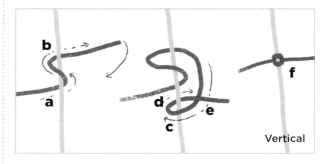

Vertical

1 To tie, draw the working strand behind the anchor (a), loop over the anchor front-to back (b), tightening to one side of the working strand.

2 Draw the working strand back to the front (c) and loop over the anchor from the other side of the hanging strand (d).

3 Then pass the end through the gap in the center from the back of the anchor (e) and tighten (f).

Diagonal Clove Hitch (DCH): This hitch procedure is the same as a clove hitch, as illustrated. The diagonal clove hitch can be right facing (DCHRF), with the anchor drawn diagonally left to right, or left facing (DCHLF), with the anchor drawn diagonally right to left.

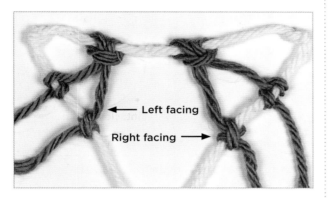

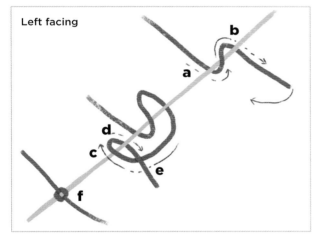

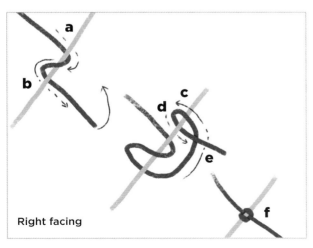

Half-Hitch (HH): On its own, the half-hitch is nothing more than a cord looped around an anchor. It's unstable; however, formed in succession, it will create a simple spiral, similar to that of the half-knot. This spiral can be left facing (HHLF), looping the working strand around an anchor or core from the right; or right facing (HHRF), looping the working strand around an anchor or core from the left.

Left: half-hitch; middle: left facing; right: right facing

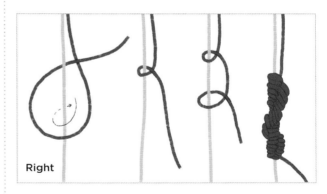

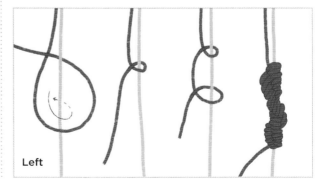

Alternate Half-Hitch (AHH): These alternate hitches form a tight bond. They are also a key knot within this book because they are so simple to form. This knot is typically formed using just two working strands in this book; however, it is often found alternating the knots around a shared core.

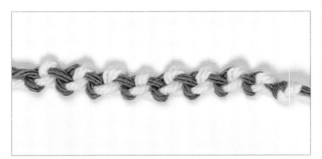

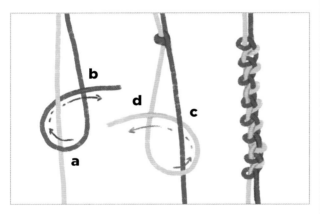

1 To form (two-strand method), loop the right strand around the left (a). Bring it back over itself (b) and tighten.

2 Repeat the process with the left strand, looping it around the right (c) and bringing it back over itself (d), and tighten.

3 Continue in this manner, alternating the colors, until you reach your desired length. This pattern is stable enough to be left on it's own, or it can be repeated in a sinnet.

Overhand Knot (OK): A very common and simple knot that can be used as a finishing knot or in an alternate pattern to form a net. Follow the same technique to tie any number of strands at once.

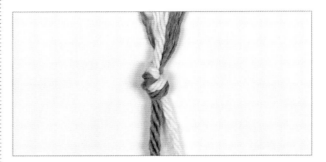

Single strand

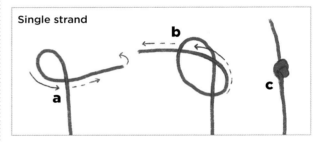

Multi-strand

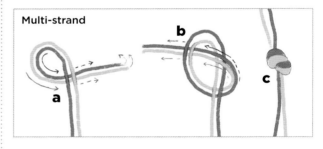

1 Form a loop into the end of the strand(s) (a).

2 Pass the end(s) through the loop (b), and tighten (c).

Half-Knot (HK): The half-knot is one half of a square knot. On its own, it is semi-unstable, so it requires either the second half of a square knot to secure, or an additional half-knot.

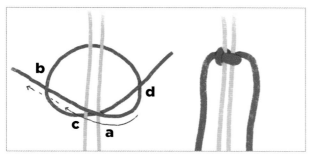

1 Draw one working strand across the core (a) and behind the other working strand (b).

2 Take the second working strand, draw it behind the core (c), and through the loop formed by the first working strand (d), then tighten.

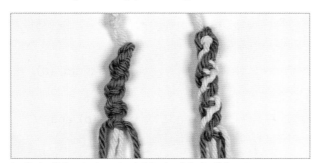

Left: half-knot sinnet; right: double half-knot

Half-Knot Sinnet (HKS): Repeating the half-knot exactly more than twice, a spiral will appear. The spiral can be left facing (HKLF) by drawing the right working strand over the core, or right facing (HKRF) by drawing the left working strand over the core.

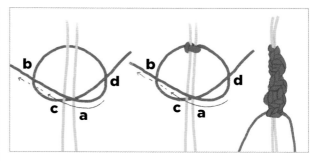

Double Half-Knot (DHK): The double spiral is a little challenging, but it is a showstopper.

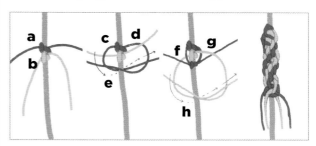

1 To form, begin by creating a half-knot with the first cord around the core (a). Set up a second half-knot directly below the first with another cord (b).

2 Skew the directions of the working strands so that the end of the first cord is on top of the second cord on the left side (c), and vice versa on the right side (d).

3 Make a half-knot with the first cord around the core (e), and tighten it so it is directly under the second cord's first knot.

4 Skew the directions of the working strands so the end of the first cord is on top of the second cord on the left side (f), and vice versa on the right side (g).

5 Make a half-knot with the second cord around the core (h), and tighten it until it is directly under the first cord's second knot.

6 Continue forming half-knots, alternating the cords.

Square Knot (SK): The square knot is a combination of a left-facing half-knot (HKLF) and right-facing half-knot (HKRF). The knot can be started from the left or right, but in the following example it is begun from the right.

1 Draw the right working strand across the core (a) and behind the left working strand (b).

2 Take the left working strand, draw it behind the core (c), and through the loop formed by the right working strand (d), and tighten.

3 Next, draw the left working strand across the core (e) and behind the right working strand (f).

4 Finally, draw the right working strand behind the core (g), through the loop formed by the left working strand (h), and tighten.

5 Repeat until you reach your desired length (i).

Alternating Square Knot (ASK): The alternating square knot can be used to form a net, the sling of a plant hanger, or a pretty panel for a wall tapestry.

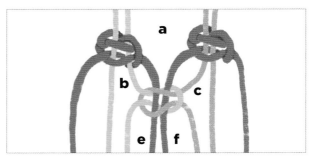

1 To form an alternate square knot, first form a row of two or more side-by-side square knots (a).

2 On the next row, the cores and working strands from the previous row swap roles to complete the next series of knots; use the right core from the left knot (b) and the left core from the right knot (c) as the working strands. The core will be built using the left working strand from left knot (e), and the right working strand from the right knot (f).

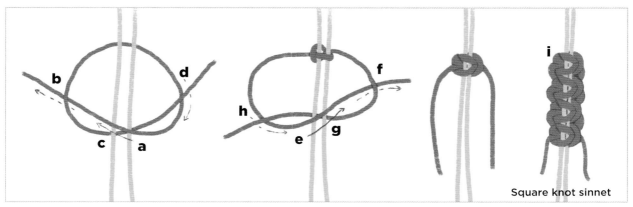

Square knot sinnet

Square knot

3 Form a square knot. Note: Any knot can be "alternated" every other row (see page 16). It basically requires shifting the position of the knots over one or two columns, or dropping one or two knots at the beginning and end of a row.

Reef Knot (RK): This is a clever little knot that is most commonly used in this book to form feathers (see page 14).

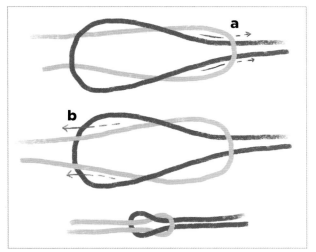

1 Find the centers of two cords.

2 Pass the ends of one strand through and under the loop of the second strand (a).

3 Feed the ends of the second strand up and through the loop of the first strand (b), then tighten.

Switch Knot (SWK): This is simply just a couple of deceptive square knots. Being with a square knot around a two-strand core. After completing this knot, sandwich the working strands between the two core strands, then draw those core strands out to act as the working strands. Form a square knot with the new working strands.

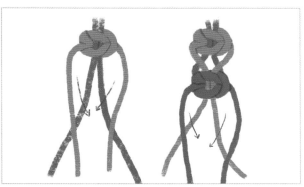

Crown Knot (CK): This knot looks trickier than it really is. It requires four strands and can be formed on its own or around a core.

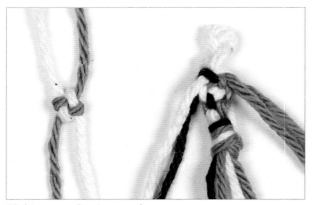

Right: crown knot around a cone

1 With the strands laid out north, east, south, and west, begin by folding the north strand over the east strand (a).

2 The east strand will fold over the north (b) and south (c) strands.

3 The south strand will fold over the east (d) and west (e) strands.

4 The west strand will fold over the south strand (f) and through the loop formed by the north strand (g).

5 Grasp all four ends and tug tight (h). Repeat the process as desired.

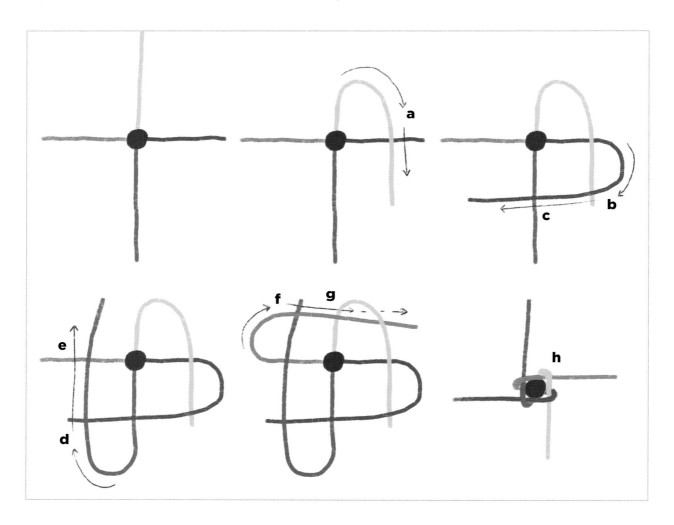

Josephine Knot (JK): Decorative on its own, this knot can be difficult to master right away, so it's best to practice before tackling this knot in a project. The Josephine knot is best thought of as a weave; think "over-under-over-under." Start with just two strands in contrasting colors for practice (the illustration shows a yellow cord and a blue cord). Multiple strands can be held side-by-side to bulk up the knot, just be sure to treat the pairs of cord as one unit.

1 To form, begin with a lowercase "b" loop with the first cord so the end pointing down is drawn to the back (a).

2 Carry the second cord over the center of the first cord's loop (b).

3 Draw the end of the second cord under the lower part of the first cord (c), and then up and over the upper part of the first cord (d).

4 Continue drawing the second cord to the right. Carry it under the upper part of the first cord's loop (e), over the part of the second cord that sits in the center of the loop (f), and then under the lower part of the first cord's loop (g).

5 Gently tug all the ends to tighten (h). This knot can be easily over-tightened, so it's best to stop when the weave is secure and visible. The same process can be applied to a multi-strand Josephine knot (second illustration below).

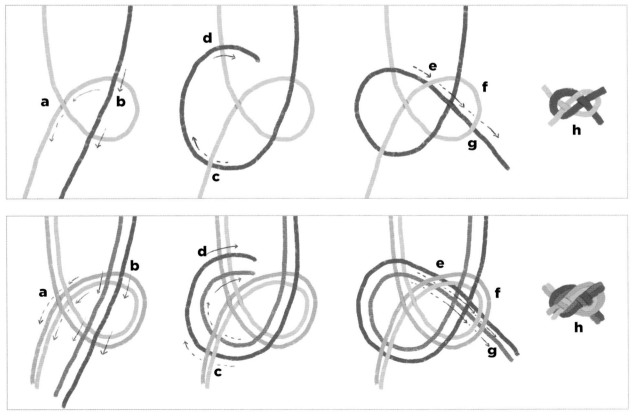

Josephine knot multiple strands

BRAIDING AND WEAVING

Three-Strand Braid (3SB): This popular braid is an easy, breezy classic. The colors red, blue, and yellow were used for this example.

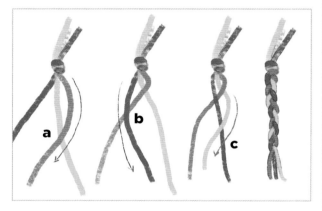

1 To form, carry the red strand over the yellow strand (a).

2 Draw the blue strand over the red strand (b).

3 Bring the yellow strand over the blue strand (c).

4 Keep repeating until you reach your desired length.

Four-Strand Flat Braid (4FB): If new to this braid, practice using four contrasting color cords.

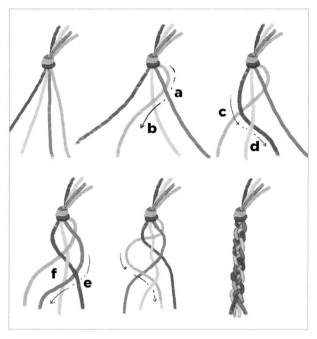

1 Draw the green strand under the red strand (a) and over the yellow strand (b).

2 Next, carry the blue strand over the green strand (c) and under the yellow strand (d).

3 Bring the red strand under the blue strand (e) and over the yellow strand (f).

4 Keep repeating this process. Your right-most strands should always go under the third strand and over the second strand, and your left-most strand should always go over the second strand and under the third.

Four-Strand Round Braid (4RB): This braid can be quite confusing at first. It is easiest to use two contrasting strands to practice, but for clarity, I recommend that you visually follow the illustration for the multi-color round braid. (When working with two colors, the set up is key; the matching strands should be side-by-side.)

1 To form this braid, carry the yellow strand behind the red and green strands (a), then up and over the red strand (b).

2 Carry the blue strand behind the red and yellow strands (c) and then over the yellow strand (d).

3 Repeat by shifting the green strand behind the yellow and blue strands (e) and then over the blue strand (f).

4 Shift the red strand behind the green and blue strands (g), then over the green strand (h). Your colors should now be in the same position as they started.

5 Continue braiding in this manner until you reach your desired length.

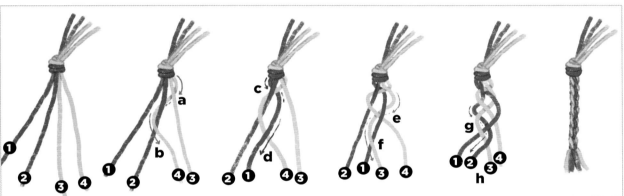

Two-color round braid

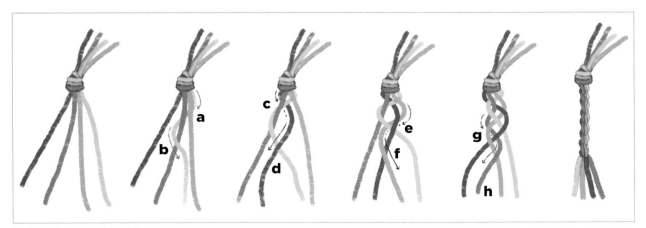

Multi-color round braid

Weaving: The basic weave requires three or more strands running horizontally, and three or more strands running vertically.

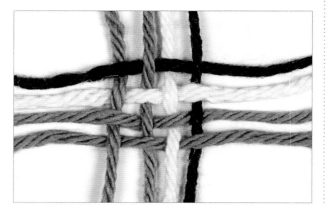

1 On the first row (and all odd rows), feed the strand over (a), under (b), over (c), under (d), etc.

2 On row two (and all even rows), feed the strand under (e), over (f), under (g), over (h), etc.

3 Tighten and compress the weave arrangement once all strands are interlaced.

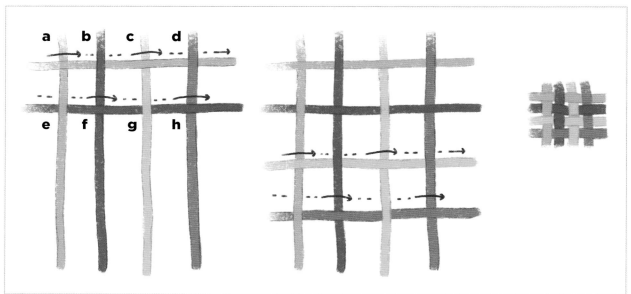

Projects

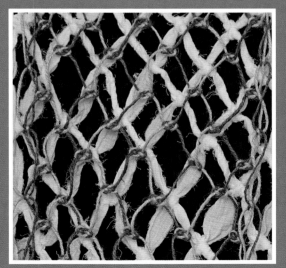

Comfy Chair

This frame is assembled using an Ikea® Poäng base; however, this design can be fitted to the chaise of your choice. The use of polypropylene cord is recommended for its indoor/outdoor stability, as well as for a level of comfort. Using a soft, braided cotton cord with dense filler may be substituted if the chair will be used inside only.

KNOTTY LEVEL: 2–3
WORKING TIME: 4 hours
FINISHED SIZES: 18¼" wide x 21¾" long (46.36 x 55.25cm)
CORDS: Polypropylene cord
SUPPLIES

- Ikea Poäng armchair frame
- Ikea Poäng lower seat cushion (no back part required)
- 512' (156.06m) of 6mm polypropylene cord: cut 16' (40.64cm)–long pieces (32 pieces total)
- Safety lighter (for cord melting)
- Pliers and sandpaper (optional)

DIRECTIONS

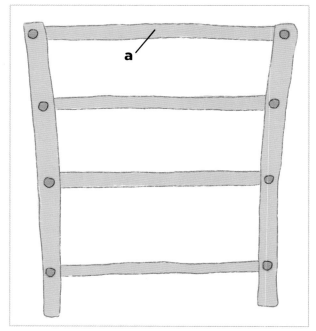

TIP: Form the back part of the chair, knot the macramé design, then finish the chair assembly. This will make the knot tying easier. Optional: If choosing to remove the staples, it will require a bit of elbow grease. Use pliers for the staple removal, and finish with a bit of sandpaper. This part will be 100% covered, so it's not a necessity.

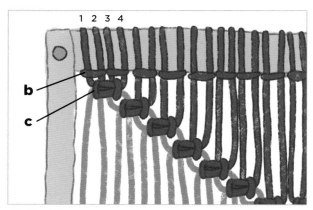

1 Assemble the armchair, following all the instructions but omitting the addition of the hook and loop strips (a).

2 Find the center of each strand of cord (32 total strands), and create lark's head knots on the top bar (b). You should have 32 total strands to start with and finish with 64 working strands at the end of this step.

3 Form four-strand square knots at the placement shown (c). Working left to right, knots positioned at: 1 to 4, 29 to 32, 33 to 36, and 61 to 64.

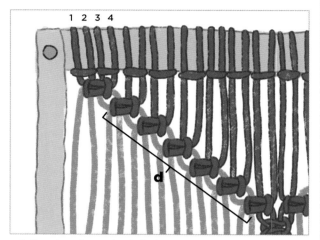

4 Starting from the left, form six right-descending alternate square knots by adding just two strands to the previous knot on the next row (d). Evenly space so the final knot settles about 1" (2.54cm) from the bar.

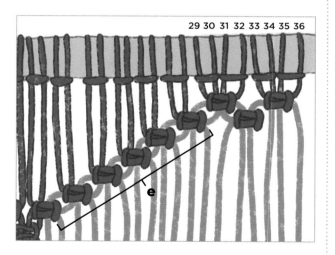

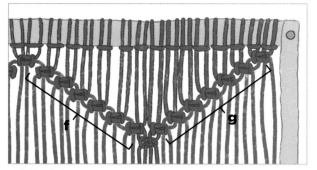

5 Find the two center square knots from the top bar. Form six left-descending alternate square knots from the left knot (e), six right-descending from the right knot (f). Repeat step 4 in reverse: Work from the top right square knot and make six left-descending alternate square knots (g). Eyeball the knots to be sure they are level.

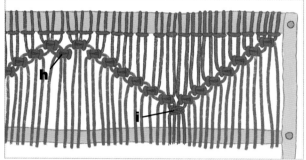

6 Form four-strand square knots joining the top center knots (h) and the two bottom points closest to the bar (i).

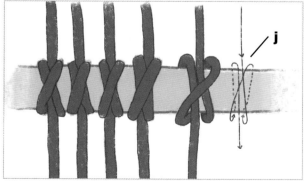

7 Working left to right, hitch each hanging strand onto the second bar, keeping the cord straight and taut (j).

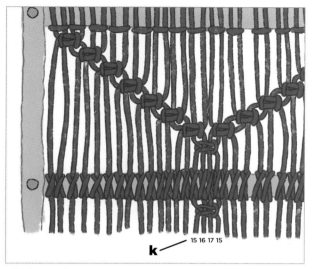

8 Steps 3 to 7 can be repeated on the next two sections if a zigzag look is desired. To make the diamond shape shown, form four-strand square knots from strands 15 to 18 and 46 to 49 (k). Repeat the same procedure as before of adding two strands to form the diagonal descending square knots. Add an extra square knot where the two center diagonal points meet.

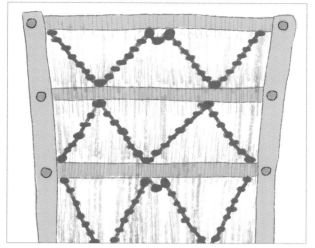

9 Repeat steps 3 to 7 on the third section.

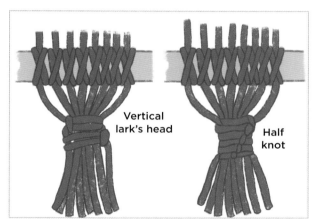

10 To finish, gather the strands below the bottom bar in groups of eight. Form two alternating vertical lark's head knots with the first and eighth strand from each group, or use these two strands to form a 2" (5.08cm)–long half-knot over the bundle. Trim and melt the ends using a safety lighter to the desired length (about 4" [10.16cm]).

11 Assemble the rest of the chair and add the seat cushion.

"Flannel" Footrest

This is a great project for knotting practice. The only trick is finding a basic ottoman or bench with basic bars across the top. This project can also be replicated across a flat table or cushioned surface.

KNOTTY LEVEL: 1–2
WORKING TIME: 4–6 hours
FINISHED SIZE: Approximately 14" x 14" (35.56 x 35.56cm) square
CORDS: 2mm cotton braid, 2mm cotton twist, or 2–4mm polypropylene or nylon cord
SUPPLIES
- 336' (102.41m) of 2mm polypropylene or nylon cord
- Woven ottoman, stool, or small accent table
- Staple gun with staples, or hammer and upholstery/carpet tacks
- Pliers (optional)
- Pencil or tape

NOTE: If a staple gun is not available, add 3' (91.44cm) to each strand and clove hitch each piece onto the wooden frame. Corner brackets will have to be ignored or temporarily removed to cover the full width and length of the stool frame. If making a larger ottoman, for each inch larger, add 4" (10.16cm) to the length of the cord.

DIRECTIONS

1 Remove any webbing or fabric from the ottoman, if necessary (a), and cut cording to required lengths.

2 Form 24 total sinnets (12 for each four-strand braid and square knot chains):
- Four-strand flat braid requires four strands at 3' (91.44cm).
- Square knot requires two strands at 6' (182.88cm) and two strands at 2' (60.96cm).
Start each chain at least 3" to 6" (7.62–15.24cm) from one end; temporarily secure this end with an overhand knot. Sinnet chains should be long enough to span the width of the stool.

3 Collect six of each of the braids and square knot chains. Arrange the pieces on top of the stool so that the square knot chains and four-strand braids alternate. Once pieces are evenly distributed across the frame, mark the position of each piece with a light pencil mark or temporarily tape each in place.

4 Untie the overhand knot from one end of each chain, then tack or staple to the underside of the footstool (b). If a piece falls out of place, refer to the marking made with the pencil for placement.

5 Turn the stool clockwise and repeat steps 3 and 4.

6 Starting from the top right corner, weave the strands together (see steps 1 and 2 on page 28). Once the arrangement of the weave is satisfactory, stretch and tack each sinnet to the bottom of the footstool (c). The resulting panel should be taut. Trim away any excess cord.

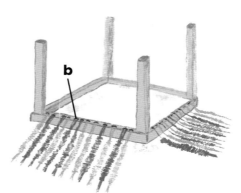

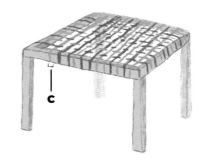

Freestanding Room Divider

The knot tying on this project is quite simple. Unless a freestanding room divider is available for knotting, it can become a bit labor intensive. To limit the cost of materials and enhance customization, this project is noted from start to finish, so it can be repeated by anyone. Room dividers are not easy to come by, nor are they inexpensive when they are available.

The look of this room divider is to still allow for light to filter through, which is great for use in a studio or kid's bedroom. If the need for a privacy screen is desired, use opaque ribbons or fabric strips. Fabric or paper can be stapled to the backside of the panels for added privacy. The patterns filling the panels are kept simple so it can be made by anyone new to the craft.

KNOTTY LEVEL: 3
WORKING TIME: Weekend+
FINISHED SIZES: 5' wide x 5' 8" tall (1.52 x 1.73m)
CORDS: Cotton yarn, ribbon, cotton cord, polypropylene or fabric strips
SUPPLIES

- (3) Ikea Ivar side unit shelf panels (20" x 70" [50.80 x 177.80cm] approximate)
- Newspaper (recommended)
- Safety glasses
- Wood hole epoxy
- Small epoxy trowel or painter's knife
- Sheet of medium-grit sandpaper
- (4) 3" (7.62cm) hinges with screws
- Screwdriver
- Drill with ⅟₁₆" (1.60mm) drill bit
- Quart of paint (desired color)
- (6) Stick-on felt pads (about 1" [2.54cm] round)
- (72) 20' (6m) strands of cotton crochet yarn (24 strands for each panel)

PANEL PRE-DIRECTIONS

1 Fill all tiny holes in the wood panels with a wood filler (available from your local hardware shop). First, take little bits of newspaper and fill in the holes as much as possible (a), then cover with the wood fill (b). The less epoxy required, the shorter the drying time. Follow the directions on the wood filler packaging to complete.

2 After the filler has dried completely, sand the panels smooth (c) and paint (d).

a b c d

3 Decide on the placement of the hinges on the center panel. Note: To create the zigzag look, the hinges on the left side need to face a different direction than those on the right. For this, measure and mark 18" (45.72cm) from the top (e) and 24" (60.96cm) from the bottom (f). Align the top/bottom edges of the hinges with the first marks, then use a pencil to mark the holes on each hinge (g). Remove the hinges and drill a shallow pilot hole (h). Screw the hinges in place on the center panel.

4 Stand the panels up side by side on a level surface (this may require helping hands). Mark the holes on the outside panels, then drill shallow pilot holes, and screw the hinges in place. Lightly sand the bottom of the divider's feet and apply the felt stickers.

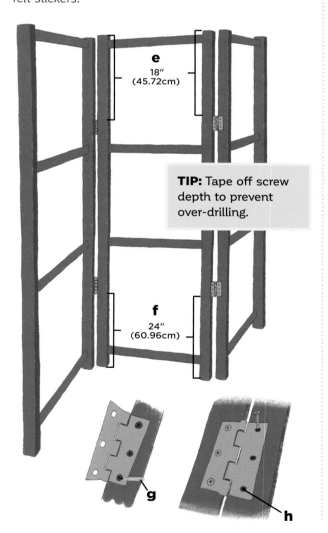

TIP: Tape off screw depth to prevent over-drilling.

KNOT TYING DIRECTIONS

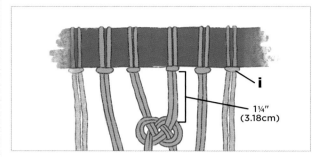

1 Find the center of each strand of yarn and knot a lark's head knot to the top of each panel (i). Arrange so that the strands are evenly distributed across the top.

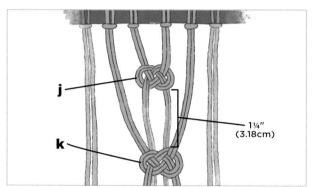

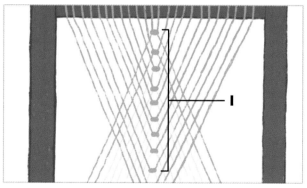

2 Starting with the center strands, pair off the strands and form a loose Josephine knot (j). The knot should sit 1¼" (3.18cm) below the frame. Continue to the next two pairs from the center. Form a loose Josephine knot, settling it 1¼" (3.18cm) below the first knot (k). Continue knotting the top portion in this pattern (l).

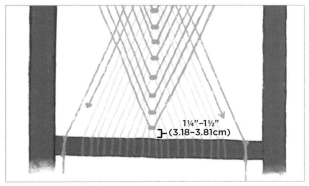

1¼"–1½"
(3.18–3.81cm)

3 The final knot should land about 1¼" to 1½" (3.18 to 3.81cm) from the crossbar. Make adjustments to the knot placements at this point if necessary. Once the spacing is even, hitch the strands to the crossbar (m). Hitch the strands from the final knot in the center and then work from the inside out, as each Josephine knot is anchored to the crossbar.

4 Repeat steps 2 and 3 for the next two sections. The middle section should have knots spaced 1⁵⁄₁₆" (3.33cm) apart, but the knots of the final section should be spaced 1⁵⁄₈" (4.14cm) apart (see illustration, right). Repeat this process for the two remaining panels.

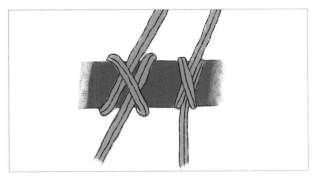

5 To finish, knot the strands to the lower bar with a cow hitch, then tie a square knot to secure (n). Add a dab of glue to the knots so they will not unravel over time. Trim away the excess yarn.

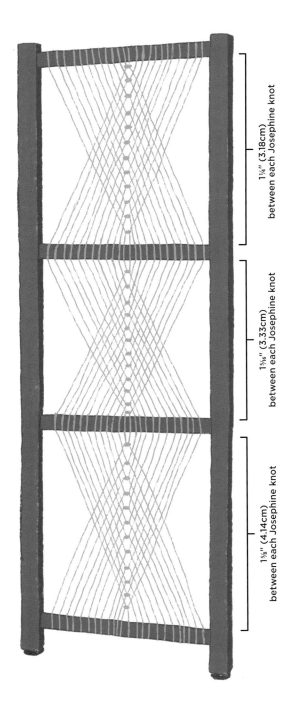

1¼" (3.18cm) between each Josephine knot

1⁵⁄₁₆" (3.33cm) between each Josephine knot

1⁵⁄₈" (4.14cm) between each Josephine knot

Granny Square Lampshade

Crochet? More like faux-chet! This macramé mock-granny square pattern converts a timeless blanket to a warming centerpiece for an accent table. This pattern is quite simple, only requiring the use of a square knot, with double lark's head to mount and clove hitches—with overhand knots—to finish. The use of a sturdy lampshade frame is recommended. While any frame can be substituted to complete this pattern, an Ängland lamp kit from Ikea is shown here.

Making a lampshade a different size? For larger frames (greater than 6" [15.24cm] at the top), add eight strands for each additional 1" (2.54cm). This will accommodate an additional mock-granny square. For smaller, subtract eight strands. For added height (greater than 8" [20.32cm] tall), measure 1' (30.48cm) for each inch (couple of centimeters) of height.

KNOTTY LEVEL: 2
WORKING TIME: 8–10 hours
FINISHED SIZE: Approximately 8" tall x 11" at the widest point (20.32 x 27.94cm)
CORDS: 2mm cotton braid, 2mm cotton twist, or 2–4mm polypropylene or nylon cord
SUPPLIES
- 572' (174.35m) of 2mm polypropylene or nylon cord
  - cut (72) 8' (2.44m)–long pieces (36 each of 2 colors)
- Lampshade (shown here, Ikea's Ängland lamp kit)
- Lamp with light bulb

DIRECTIONS

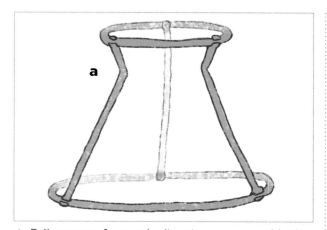

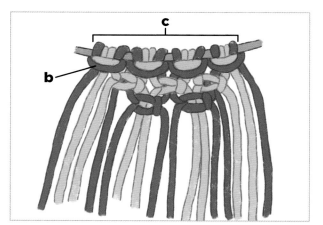

1 Follow manufacturer's directions to assemble the lamp and lampshade frame. If using a pre-made lampshade, remove the material exposing the wire frame (a).

2 Mount two strands at a time to the top ring of the lampshade using a double lark's head knot (b). Consistently mount the cord with the same color in the center.

3 Each granny square is worked within the cords from four lark's head knot groups (c). Select a group next to a frame joint as a starting point:

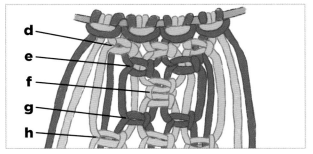

Row 1: Skip the first two strands, form three square knots, and leave the last two strands (d).

Row 2: Skip four strands, form two square knots, and leave the last four strands (e).

Row 3: Skip six strands, form two complete square knots in a single sinnet, and skip the last six strands (f).

Row 4: Repeat row 2 (g).

Row 5: Repeat row 1 (h).

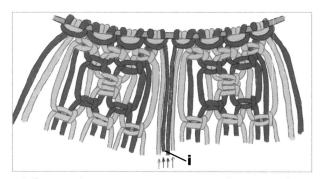

4 Repeat the granny square pattern from step 3 around the circumference of the lampshade. Remember to skip the first two strands from each group of cords (i). There will be a total of nine finished granny squares.

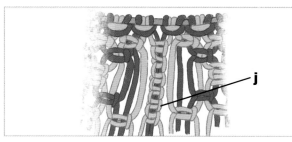

5 Returning to those four strands between the granny squares, form six square knots in a single sinnet (j). The sixth square knot should align with the final row of square knots from the granny squares.

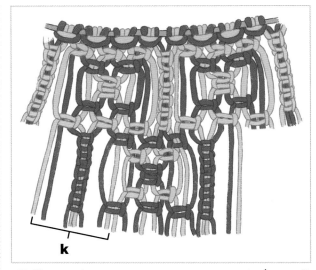

6 Repeat the granny square pattern again (steps 3 to 5), but first shift the placement of the square over by eight strands (k). There will be nine finished granny squares.

7 Form two more rows of granny squares, following steps 3 to 6. Fill in the gap to the ring with a row (or two if necessary) of square knots.

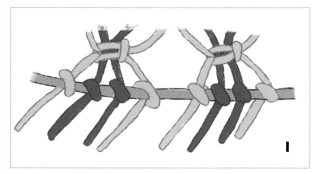

8 To finish, tie each strand to the bottom ring from the inside with a clove hitch. Then evenly trim the strands so that each is roughly ½" to ¾" (1.27 to 1.91cm) long. Ends can be either melted or tightened with an overhand knot to prevent fray.

Chalkboard Hanging Tray

Here we have a fringe-free hanger. This tray holder is clean and simple, but the Josephine knots pump up the "pretty" by imitating little bows. In this project, I used a braided cotton and dip-dyed the base to accent the wood of the tray a bit more.

KNOTTY LEVEL: 2
WORKING TIME: 1–2 hours
FINISHED SIZE: 36" (91.44cm) long
CORDS: Cotton, parachute cord, polypropylene, jute
SUPPLIES

- Ring (metal or wooden)
- 10"–14" (25.40–35.56cm)–wide tray, either rectangular or square in shape
- (4) 12' (3.66m) pieces of 3–6mm cord
- Little dab of glue
- Rubber band (optional)

DIRECTIONS

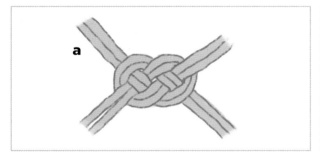

1 Find the center of the cords and form a large Josephine knot (a).

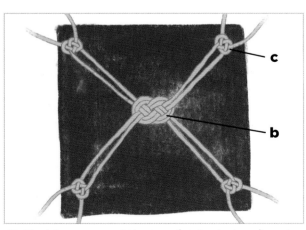

2 Find the center of the tray (at the bottom) and measure out from the corners (b). Set Josephine knots in each corner (c). Be sure each knots are set at an equal distance from the center.

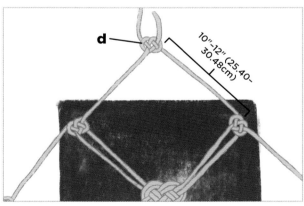

3 Draw the cords out to form an alternate Josephine knot with its neighboring group (d). The knots should be set 10" to 12" (25.4 to 30.48cm) from the previous set of knots. Measure the placement carefully so that you're sure the tray will sit level.

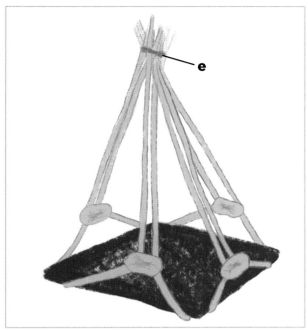

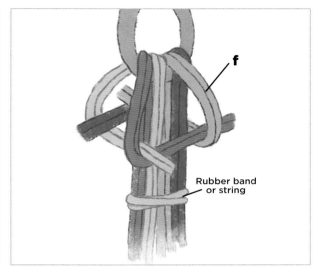

Rubber band or string

4 Flip the tray upright. Draw the cords straight up until they are all taut and the tray is floating level. Gather and band the cords to keep them from slipping (e). Fold the pairs of cord into the ring. Two pairs should be entering the ring in one direction, and two pairs in the other. You will want to have about 18" to 20" (45.72 to 50.80cm) of overhang.

5 Recommend setting a rubber band just below the ring so that the cords don't slide or slack as you work this first row. Working clockwise around the ring, fold the pairs of cord to the other side of the ring to weave the crown knot (f).

6 The rubber band can be removed after the first crown knot is completed. Check the tray to be sure it's still level, and tighten the knot as much as possible. Form as many rows of the crown knot as you can. When you've run out of cord, tighten and trim the ends. Glue can be applied to the cut points to prevent fray.

Optional: Dip-dye to embellish.

Hanging Photo Gallery

Form and function come together to make a pretty dorm room delight. The idea is that this frame can be used as a simple piece of room decor on its own, or photos and jewelry can be tacked to it for a little personalization. This is a visually stunning project for knot practice.

KNOTTY LEVEL: 2
WORKING TIME: 6 hours
FINISHED SIZE: 18" wide x 24" long (45.72 x 60.96cm)
CORDS: Worsted weight yarns, 1mm leather, 1mm satin rattail cord
SUPPLIES

- (20) 2½' (76.20cm) lengths of cotton crochet yarn
- (4) 20' (6.10m) lengths of cotton crochet yarn
- (4) 8' (2.44m) lengths of cotton crochet yarn
- Approximately 100' (30.48m) of cotton crochet yarn for feathers
- Macramé board with T-pins (recommended)
- Glue
- (12+) Mini binder clips or decorative paper clips
- (4+) Clear plastic micro wall mount clips or wall tacks

DIRECTIONS

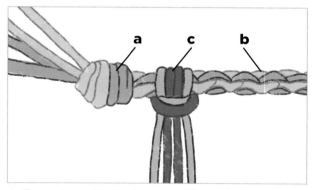

1 Beginning with the horizontal bars, tie four lengths of the 2½' (76.20cm) cords together with an overhand knot (a) settled 3" (7.62cm) from one end. Proceed to create an 18" (45.72cm) four-strand braid (b) then finish with another overhand knot. Make a total of five horizontal pieces.

2 Find the centers of one 8' (2.44m) length of yarn (shown as blue in the illustration) and one 20' (6.10m) length of yarn (shown as green in the illustration), and tie a double lark's head knot to the end of one of the finished braids (c). The blue yarn needs to be in the center to act as the core for the square knots made with the green yarn.

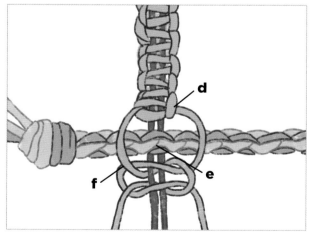

3 Square knot for 6" (15.24cm) (see top of page 48). To add the next horizontal bar, begin the first half of a square knot (d), slip the braided rope so it sits in front of the core (e). Complete the other half of the square knot (f) then tighten. Continue forming another 6" (15.24cm) sinnet of square knots, repeating this procedure until all five braided pieces have been mounted. Finish the last mount with a square knot, followed by an overhand knot.

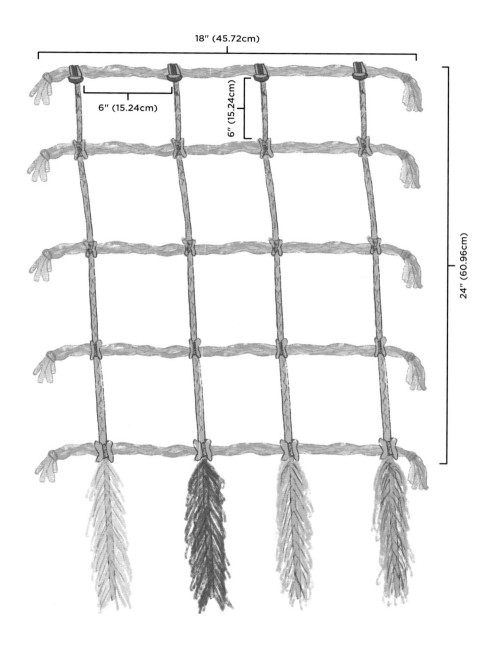

18" (45.72cm)

6" (15.24cm)

6" (15.24cm)

24" (60.96cm)

4 Repeat steps 2 and 3 for the next three vertical mounts, spacing each bar 6" (15.24cm) apart.

5 Finish by forming feathers at the base of the hanging and trimming the side tassels to 3" (7.62cm). Each feather here is formed using 24' (7.32m) of yarn cut into 6" (15.24cm) segments (see page 14).

6 The frame can be hung from a wall with tacks or removable clear micro wall clips. Use mini binder clips or decorative paper clips to add pictures and light ornaments to the frame.

Pillow Coverlet

Sink into your pillow. It's dreamy! This lovely design is set up to be repeated across the full front of a Euro-style pillow. The design can be spread or compressed down to fill just about any scale pillow. A 20" (50.80cm) square pillow was chosen for this project, as it is a comfortable size for a decorative pillow that can double as a floor cushion.

KNOTTY LEVEL: 2–3
WORKING TIME: 3 hours
FINISHED SIZE: 20" x 20" (50.80 x 50.80cm) square
CORDS: Cotton crochet yarn, worsted weight yarn
SUPPLIES

- Ball of cotton crochet yarn cut:
  - (20) 12' (3.66m) length pieces
  - (1) 8' (2.44m)–long piece
  - (5) 4' (1.22m)–long pieces
  - (2) 12'–16' (3.66–4.88m) pieces (for sewing)
- Cardboard
- Crochet hook (optional)
- Large-eyed needle with extra yarn
- 20" x 20" (50.8 x 50.8cm) pillow

DIRECTIONS

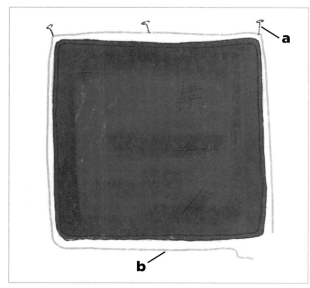

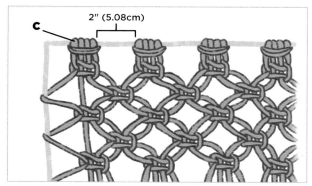

1 Align the 8' (2.44m) piece of yarn with the perimeter of the pillow, pinning it to a piece of cardboard as you go (a). Be sure to leave the bottom loose (b).

2 Mount the 20 strands onto the top edge of the anchor strand with double lark's head knots (c). These knots should be spaced 2" (5.08cm) apart.

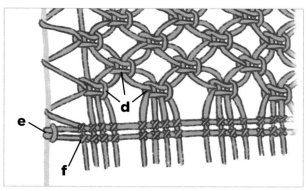

3 Form five rows of alternating square knots (d). Find the center of one 4' (1.22m) strand of yarn, and mount to the left anchor with a lark's head knot to form a horizontal anchor (e). Clove or cow hitch each hanging strand to each of the two horizontal anchors (f).

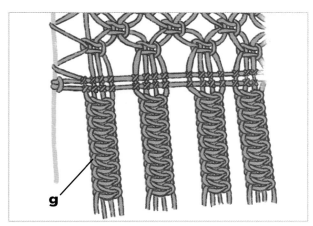

4 Next section: Group the strands into four and form eight square knots in a sinnet (g). This row will have a total of ten sinnets. Finish this row with a 4' (1.22m) anchor strand, and clove or cow hitch each piece to the horizontal anchor.

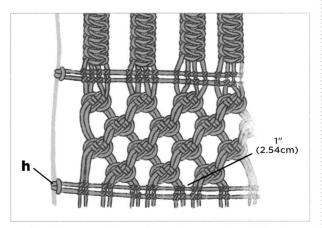

5 Third section: Form four alternate Josephine knot rows and finish with another 4' (1.22m) anchor (h). The Josephine knots should be spaced about 1" (2.54cm) apart. At this point, the pattern should be 10" long by 10" wide (25.40 by 25.40cm).

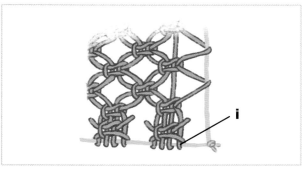

6 Finish off the pillow by mirroring the previous sections: step 5, then step 4, and then step 3. To finish, draw the perimeter anchor cord across the bottom, and mount the hanging strands to the anchor by clove or cow hitching four strands to the anchor at a time, and finishing with a square knot (i). The anchor strands can be loosely tied together.

TIP: It may be easiest to turn the project upside down to perform step 6.

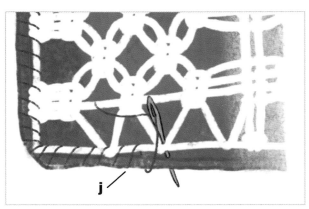

7 Using extra yarn and a large-eyed needle, sew the perimeter anchor to the outside of the pillow with a whipstitch (j).

Geometric Window Valance

This window valance is designed to fit a single window opening. To make adjustments to the width, add or subtract a section (14 strands) to enlarge the piece so it's suitable for double-window opening. Using a macramé valance will allow tons of light to come through in your room, while still adding warmth and flair to the décor. Make multiples for a room with more than one window.

KNOTTY LEVEL: 2–3
WORKING TIME: 12–24 hours (weekend project)
FINISHED SIZE: 18" tall x 5' wide
  (45.72 x 152.40cm)
CORDS: 4–6mm polypropylene or nylon cord, braided or twisted cotton rope
SUPPLIES
  • (48) 12' (3.66m) strands of 6mm polypropylene (color A)
  • (7) 15' (4.57m) strands of 6mm polypropylene cord (color B)
  • (1) 20' (6.10m) strands of 6mm polypropylene cord (color B)
  • Drapery rod with finials and mounting kit (rod should be able to expand to 60" [1.52m])
  • Crochet hook (optional)

DIRECTIONS

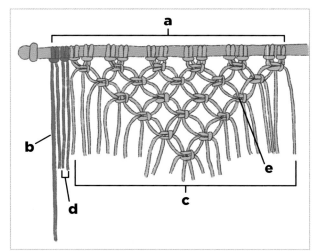

1 Mount and suspend the cord onto the drapery rod using lark's head knots (a). The 20' (6.10m) strand (b) is mounted to one end; offset the lark's head knot so the strands hang long on the outside (about 7' to 8' [2.13 to 2.44m] inside, remaining 11' to 12' [3.35 to 3.66m] hanging on the outside). Hang the rest of the cords in a pattern of twelve 12' (3.66m) strands (c) and two 15' (4.57m) strand pieces (d) on either side of that section. There will be only one 15' (4.57m) strand suspended at the end.

2 Form a row of square knots from the 12' (3.66m) strand sections (e). Form a descending point by dropping the first two and last two strands on each row to form alternating square knots. The final row will contain one square knot.

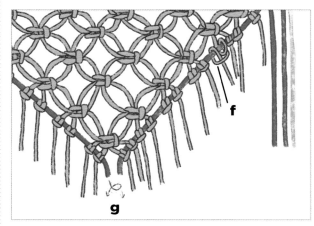

3 Draw the adjacent contrasting strand along the triangular shape formed by square knots. Tie a series of cow hitches to the hanging strands to create a diagonal edge (f). Form a Josephine knot in the center where the diagonal strands meet (g).

Psst!
This project can be easily converted into a floating headboard. Make it as directed to fit a full- to queen-size bed. To make the piece suitable for a twin- or king-size bed, subtract or add a section (14 strands).

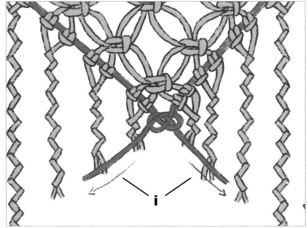

5 Draw the two contrasting strands out away from the center at a diagonal (i), and double hitch each strand onto the cord.

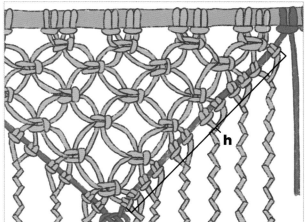

4 Pair off the strands and form a series of alternating half-hitches (h). Working from the center out, columns contain: 3 knots, 7 knots, 13 knots, 17 knots, 23 knots, and 27 knots.

TIP: On the left side of the section, form half-hitches from **right to left**. On the right side of the section, form half-hitches from **left to right**. This will help accentuate the descending angle.

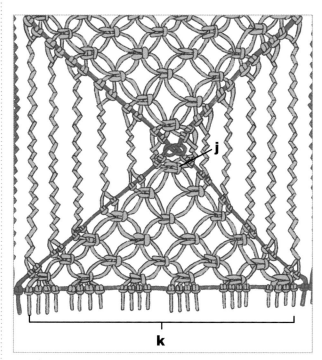

6 Returning to the center of the section, form a square knot (j). For each row, add two strands and continue the alternating pattern until there are six rows (k).

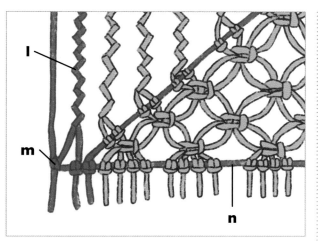

7 Repeat steps 2 to 6 for each of the remaining three sections. Between each section, tie alternate half-hitches to the loose contrasting strands until the knotted column is even with the bottom of the knotted sections (l).

8 Tie alternate half-hitches to the two ends so they are square (m). Draw the long strand across the bottom of the project, and tie double clove hitches to each cords' end (n). At the end of the row, draw the line back across the bottom and continue hitching the cord to the bottom to form a second row. Finish with an alternating half-hitch.

9 The ends can be trimmed evenly into a fringe, or use a hook to weave the ends into the back of the project. Mount above a window.

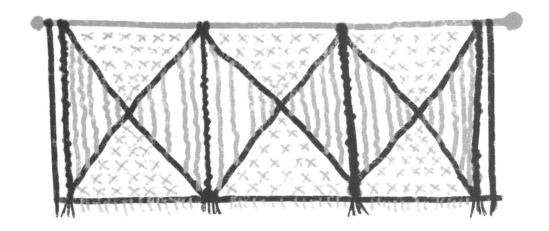

Tassel Reading Nook

The base for this project was assembled using the Rullen light fixture from Ikea; however, this design can be fitted to a Hula-Hoop® if the addition of a light is not desired. This project is a great substantial-looking project for a beginner because it only requires two knots to form the hanging tassels: the wrap and square knot. The rest of the project relies on basic crafting skills, such as measuring, grommet hammering, and minor sewing (if desired).

KNOTTY LEVEL: 1–2
WORKING TIME: 4 hours
FINISHED SIZE: 7½'–8' (2.29–2.44m) long
CORDS: Yarns (acrylic or cotton)
SUPPLIES

- 18" (46cm) Rullan light fixture (metal ring or Hula-Hoop can be substituted if the nook will not be used with lighting)
- Hanging lamp kit (Hemma from Ikea shown) with light bulb
- 5–6 yd. (4.57–5.49m) of sheer, semi-sheer, or lace fabric (at least 50' [1.27m] wide)
- Pins (recommended)
- (4–6) Skeins of cotton or acrylic yarn, worsted weight
- (40) ⁵⁄₃₂" (4mm) metal grommets
- Hammer (for grommets)
- Sewing machine or needle and thread (optional)
- Ceiling hooks (this may come with the lamp kit)

DIRECTIONS

1 Cut the fabric so that there are two 7½' to 8' (2.29 to 2.44m) pieces (cut the bolt fabric in half). Optional: Sew the two panels together on one side. Allow a ¼" (0.64cm) seam allowance.

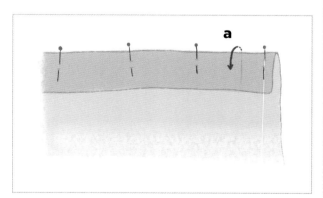

2 Fold down the top edge (about 1" [2.54cm]) and apply pins to keep it steady (a). Arrange the pins so that there are at least 20 evenly spaced along both panels.

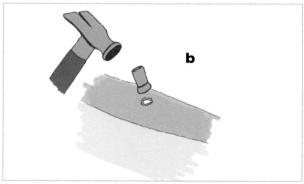

3 Apply the grommets (follow package directions) by snipping a tiny hole into the fabric, about ¾" (1.91cm) from the folded end, add a grommet, and hammer down flat (b).

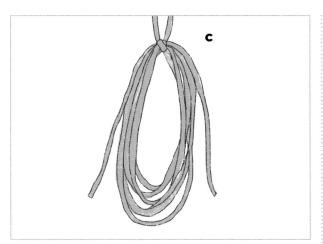

4 Set the panels aside and form the base of 40 tassels (see page 15). Wrap a piece of yarn around four fingers about 20 times, or when the preferred fullness is achieved. Add a 12" (30.48cm) piece of matching yarn to the top center and tie off with a square knot, leaving the ends of this hanging strand untied. Stop here; do not wrap or trim the tassels yet (c).

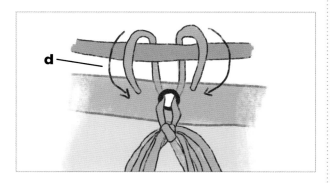

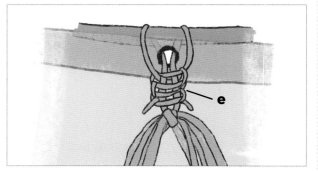

5 Start from one end of the fabric panel. Thread a tassel through a grommet, passing the strands up behind the ring, over top the ring (d), and finally form a series of two to three square knots around

the strands, to tack the tassel in place (e). Repeat across the full lamp frame. There should be ten tassels tied into each quadrant.

> **TIP:** Crisscross the tassel ties at the spokes, except for the final tassel, so that the curtain can be drawn side to side. This will keep the weight of the curtain well distributed, as well as stable.

6 Wrap each one of the tassels using contrasting color yarn. Be sure to capture the hanging strands used to tie the tassels to the ring. The wrap strands should be about 12" (30.48cm) long. Trim and cut the loops of the tassels so the ends are even. Optional: A dab of clear-drying craft glue can be applied to the cut point on the wrap to prevent the wrap from unraveling over time.

7 Attached the lamp kit to the center of the ring, then suspend from the ceiling.

Tutu Chandelier

This project was inspired by capiz shell and tassel chandeliers I've seen in luxury resorts and home furnishing stores. The ribbony waves of the untwisted cotton offer a texture of natural sea grass. Paired with the trendy inverted tier, this project has a timeless shabby chic vibe, which will match a boho room décor for years to come.

I chose to use a soft blush pink color for this project. Though this can be replicated in any color imaginable, I recommend cream, mint, and soft corals for this pallet, to keep that feminine, mermaid appeal.

KNOTTY LEVEL: 2
WORKING TIME: 8–12 hours
FINISHED SIZE: 10" round x 12" tall (25.40 x 30.48cm)
CORDS: Yarns, cotton string or twine
SUPPLIES

- Portable lamp kit
- Light bulb
- 8" (20.32cm) metal ring
- Lampshade, at least 10" (25.40cm) at the top (**NOTE:** I saved the 15" [38.10cm] lower ring for the Cotton Candy Dream Catcher on page 119)
- Approximately 140 yd. (128.02m) cotton crochet yarn in color of your choice (measures about ⅛" [0.32cm] diameter)
- Macramé brush (recommended)

DIRECTIONS

1 Cut the cotton yarn into 12" (30.48cm) pieces. This will take a while! In the end, you'll need 240 pieces for the larger ring and 176 pieces for the smaller ring. The way I did this was to pile eight pieces together for each triangle formation on the rings so that they were ready to grab and easy to count.

2 Take apart the lampshade. I only used the top portion of the lamp and set the larger base aside to use for a future dream catcher project.

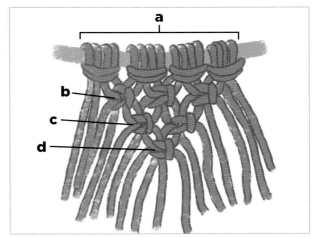

3 Use a double lark's head knot to tie each of the pieces onto the rings as follows: Mount 176 pieces onto the 8" (20.32cm) ring; mount 240 pieces onto the 10" (25.40cm) ring. Note: I recommend mounting eight pieces (four complete double lark's head knots) at a time (a) and then following the knot-tying process (step 4). This will make the detail work easier to organize and follow.

4 Starting with either ring, form three alternate square knots (b). Drop down one row and form two alternating square knots (c). Then drop down one row and form one square knot (d). Repeat around the circumference of the ring.

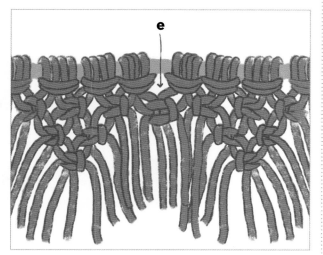

5 Working around the perimeter of the ring, use a square knot to tie the sections together (e); this will prevent the cord from slipping through the lark's head knots. I do this last because it keeps the sections separated and easier to organize.

6 Untwist the strands of yarn and comb them through with your fingers, or use a macramé brush to fluff out the fringe. When using the brush, comb with delicate strokes, starting at the bottom of the strand and working your way up toward the knots.

7 Repeat steps 4 to 6, to mount and knot cord onto the remaining ring.

Want to make this project bigger? For each 1″ (2.54cm) diameter larger, add sixteen strands (eight double lark's head knots) to keep the ring covered in full.

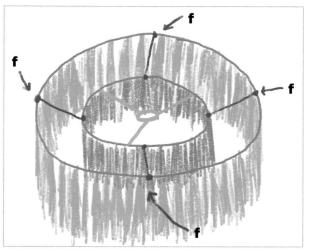

8 Center the 8″ (20.32cm) ring inside the 10″ (25.40cm) ring. Using four to six pieces of yarn, tie the rings together (f). Check the balance of the 8″ (20.32cm) ring by holding the 10″ (25.40cm) ring level.

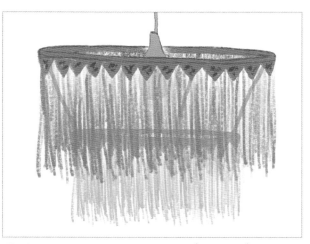

9 Attach the lamp kit to the 10″ (25.40cm) ring and add the light bulb. Hang and turn on your lovely work of art!

TIP: I recommend going to your local home improvement store for the lampshade and kit. Most will have the corresponding parts for this easy-to-assemble project.

Honeycomb Mat

This chunky, rose gold mat is a great way to dress up any tabletop. The cord I used had a bunch of soft colors that blended beautifully together. The holey pattern is a fun design that adds interest to any décor. Although this mat is perfectly sized for a coffee table, you may consider doubling its size to be used as a rug by your front door.

KNOTTY LEVEL: 1–2
WORKING TIME: 6 hours
FINISHED SIZE: 24" x 16" (60.96 x 40.64cm)
CORDS: 4 mm jute or 4–6 mm polypropylene cord
SUPPLIES
- 278' (84.73m) of 6mm polypropylene cord cut into:
- (1) 38' (11.58m) length (perimeter piece)
- (10) 24' (7.32m) lengths
- Small crochet hook or piece of floral wire formed into a hook
- Cork or foam board (at least 2' x 3' [60.96 x 91.44cm] wide) with T-pins

DIRECTIONS

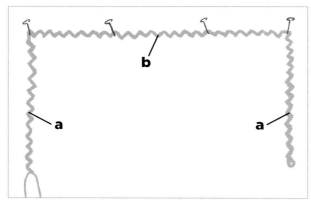

1 Starting with the perimeter of the mat, fold the 38' (11.58m) piece of cord in half and knot a chain of alternating half-hitches. The final length of this chain should be 56" (1.42m): two short sides (a) and one long side (b).

TIP: Form infinity bundles (see page 6) to keep the long lengths under control.

2 Tack the half-hitch strip down into the partial rectangle as shown above. The remaining cord will be knotted when forming the final row.

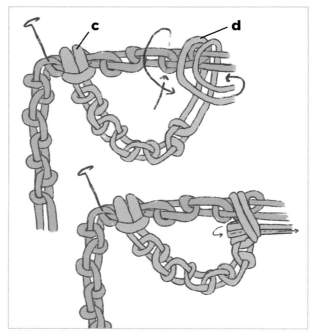

3 Take one 24' (7.32m) piece of cord and fold it in half. Tie a lark's head knot to one corner of the mat (c). Form eight alternate half-hitches, loop to the top of the mat from the back (d), and repeat across the width of the mat to complete this row. Ends will be woven back into the mat when completed.

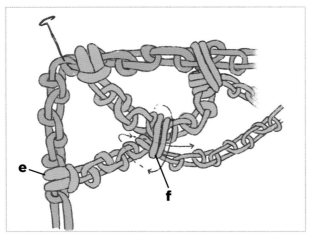

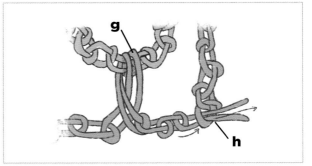

4 On the next row, take another strand of cord and tie a lark's head knot to the vertical edge of the mat, parallel to the bottom of the first loop (e). Form four alternate half-hitches, then hitch to the bottom of the first loop (f). Continue across this row, forming eight alternating half-hitches, then tacking to the bottom of the scale from the previous row.

5 Repeat the process of rows 1 and 2 (steps 3 and 4) for the remainder of the mat (seven additional rows; see below) until the final row.

6 To form the final row, return to the perimeter hanging strand and form four alternating half-hitches, then bind with the bottom peak of the previous row (g). Continue with forming eight alternating half-hitches, then binding, across the row, ending with just four knots at the end.

7 To finish, pass the ends through the bottom of the perimeter weave (h). Tie off with an alternating half-hitch, tuck and trim, and melt (with polypropylene cord only) the cut ends if desired. This mat may require some blocking (keep it tacked up on a board for a day or longer) to settle its shape.

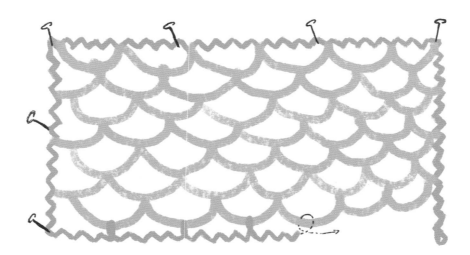

Patch Scrap Mat

This fun and colorful rug is the perfect way to use up those scraps from your fabric stash. The beauty of this mat is in the random use of fabric pieces; there is no set pattern that can be found in the prints I used. I like the frayed look to the fabric, too, so I just use straight cuts and let it go! If you wanted something a little more decorative (and to reduce the fraying), use pinking shears to give the edges of the fabric scraps a zigzag design.

KNOTTY LEVEL: 2
WORKING TIME: 3 hours
FINISHED SIZE: 30" x 18" (76.20 x 45.72cm)
CORDS: Scrap fabric or ribbon
SUPPLIES
- Roughly 250'–300' (76.20–91.44m) of scrap fabric pieces, each 1"–1½" (2.54–3.81cm) wide
- 9' x 1" (274.32 x 2.54cm) length of fabric (or ribbon, or several pieces of fabric tied together)
- Crochet hook or wire hook made from a paper clip
- Macramé board with T-pins (optional)
- 30" x 18" (76.20 x 45.72cm) non-slip mat (optional)

DIRECTIONS

1 Using the 9' (2.74m)–long fabric strip, pin it into a 30" by 18" (76.20 by 45.72cm) rectangle (onto a large surface or macramé board, if possible). Allow at least a 6" (15.24cm) overhang at the beginning and end so that these pieces can be tied together (a).

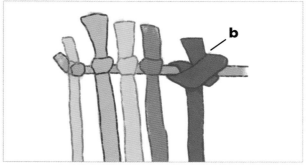

2 Mount 40 pieces to the top of the rectangle with a clove hitch (b).

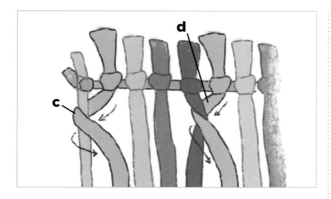

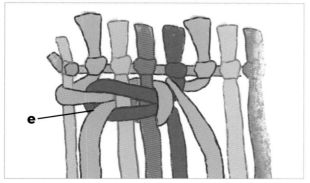

3 Beginning from the left, wrap the first piece of fabric around the left edge of the rectangle (c). Crisscross strips 4 and 5 (d), then proceed to form a square knot with four hanging pieces of fabric (e).

4 Continue twisting the fourth and fifth pieces and tie square knots across the full row. At the end of the row, wrap the last piece of fabric around the right edge and form the final square knot.

TIP: Pin each row as you complete them to keep the mat straight.

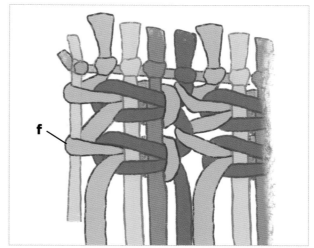

5 Repeat steps 3 and 4 to fill in the mat (f). As pieces shorten, add more fabric to the end (see page 12).

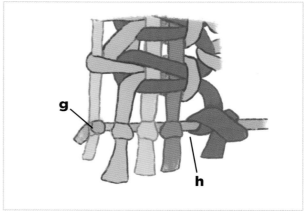

6 To finish, tie in a new bottom anchor piece (g). Tie clove hitches with each piece of fabric to the bottom of the new anchor piece (h). Use a hook to weave ends into the underside of the mat if a finished edge is desired (I left mine loose). Set the mat on a non-slip pad if you plan on using it as a welcome mat.

Small Lattice Weave Mat

Stripes are always a great design for any décor. This mat looks best when using contrasting colors. I chose to use a palette of lavender and gray, but if you wanted to go a little bolder, black and white colors are always a classy choice.

KNOTTY LEVEL: 1–2
WORKING TIME: 8–12 hours
FINISHED SIZE: 2' x 1' (60.96 x 30.48cm)
CORDS: Super bulky weight 6mm polypropylene, 4–5mm jute, or super bulky yarn.
(Do not use smooth cords for this project; the half-hitches will not hold.)
SUPPLIES

- 339' (103.33m) of 6mm polypropylene cord: cut into 2 pieces at 3' (91.44cm) (color A) and 48 pieces at 5' (152.4cm) (36 pieces from color A, 12 from color B)
- Large macramé board or pinning surface (recommended)
- (12) T-pins
- Crochet hook (size N or Q) or a paper clip formed into a hook
- Anti-slip mat 1½' x 2' (45.72 x 60.96cm) with sewing needle and thread (optional)
- Safety lighter (optional)

DIRECTIONS

1 Tie an overhand knot in one end of 3' (91.44cm) strands of cord. Leave roughly 3" (7.62cm) overhang. Pin to a board and mount all 48 pieces of cord onto the 3' (91.44cm) mount using a clove hitch. Pattern: Mount twelve pieces of color A (a), then four pieces of color B (b), six color A (c), four color B (d), six color A (e), four color B (f), and twelve color A (g). Reserve the remaining 3' (91.44cm) strand for the end of the mat.

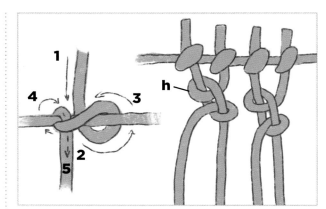

2 Form a full row of two alternating half-hitches (h).

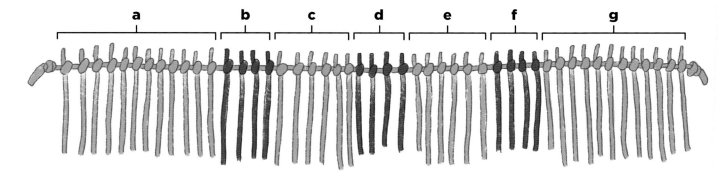

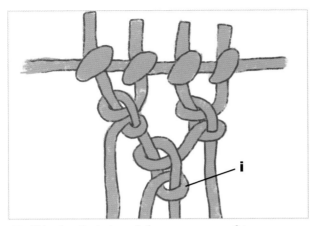

3 Skip the first strand, form one row of two alternating half-hitches, then skip the final strand (i). Repeat this pattern until the mat reaches 18" (45.72cm) long, ending on an odd row.

4 Tie an overhand knot into one end of the 3' (91.44cm) strand. Mount each strand to the 3' (91.44cm) piece of cord using the clove hitch. Lay the mat on a flat surface and adjust so that it's straight. Tie overhand knots into the end of the two 3' (91.44cm) mounting strands, flush against the end of the mat.

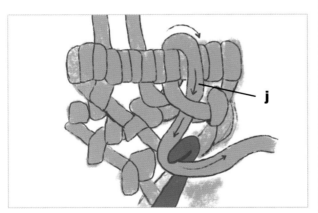

5 Turn the project to the back and weave all ends into the mat (j). Trim excess cord and melt the ends with a lighter to prevent fray (optional; for polypropylene or nylon cords only).

6 Optional: Sew a traction mat to the underside to prevent slippage when using this mat on smooth floor surfaces. This will also add some stability.

WANT TO INCREASE THE SCALE OF THIS PROJECT?

1. Determine the size of your mounting (and final anchor) cord: add about 6" to 10" (15.24 to 25.40cm) to the final width of the desired mat. For a 4' by 6' (1.22 by 1.83cm) mat, two strands at roughly 80" (2.03m) long (around 6½' [1.98m]) will be needed.
2. Using the 6mm cord, 1" (2.54cm) = 2 strands. Take the width of the mat in inches (centimeters) and multiply by 2. Example: a 6' (1.83m)-wide mat is 72" (182.88cm) = 144 strands.
3. To determine the mat length, cut cords 4.5 x desired length in feet (meters). Example: a 4' (1.22m)-long mat will be 4' (1.22m) x 4.5 = 18' (5.49m).
4. For the weaving strands in 2mm cord, two pieces will be required for each alternate row; length equals 1.5 x the width in feet (meters). For the 6' (1.83m)-wide mat, each strand will be 6' (1.83m) x 1.5 = 9' (2.74m) in length.

Ultra-Plush Mat

This mat is an excellent way to soften up any room's décor. You could also consider placing it by your bed. Imagine sinking your toes into this plush number first thing in the morning.

Is this mat cozy? Oh yes! Is it easy to make? Absolutely. This project only requires the mastery of one knot: the Josephine. This knot can be a little difficult to manage in sinnet form for a beginner, but once practiced, this rug is easy to master.

KNOTTY LEVEL: 1–2
WORKING TIME: 8–12 hours
FINISHED SIZE: Approximately 2' x 4' (60.96 x 121.92cm)
CORDS: Ultra-bulky acrylic weight yarns
SUPPLIES

- About 100 yd. (91.44m) ultra-thick acrylic yarn (¾"–1" [1.91–2.54cm] round)
- Crochet hook (optional)

DIRECTIONS

1 Cut the yarn into nine pieces at 16' (4.88m) lengths each, and seven at 19' (5.79m) lengths each.

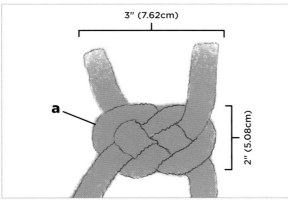

2 Form one Josephine knot using two 16' (4.88m) strands of the yarn. This knot should sit about 2" (5.08cm) from the end. Each knot should measure 2" tall by 3" wide (5.08 by 7.62cm) (a).

TIP: If any strands have been tied together, these bulky knots can be easily concealed in the middle of a knot.

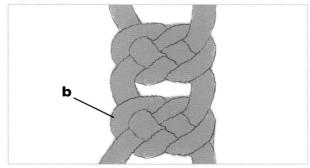

3 Continue forming a sinnet of Josephine knots (b) until a length of 4' (121.92cm) or 50" (127cm) is achieved.

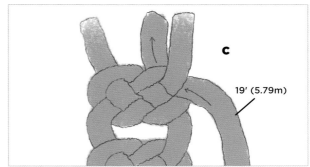

4 Gather the next two strands: one 19' and 16' (5.79 and 4.88m) in length. Thread the 19' (5.79m) strand into the first formed Josephine knot, then tie the two core ends together (c). This will secure and stitch the two side-by-side sinnets.

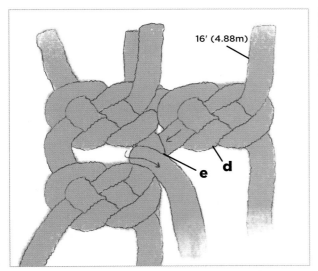

5 Form the first Josephine knot on this column (d). Before forming the second knot, thread the left (the longer) strand through the second knot from the first column (e).

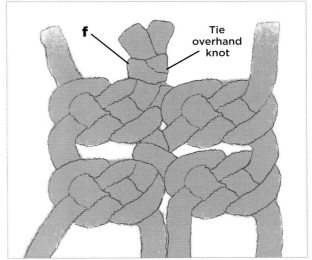

6 Repeat this pattern until the throw measures 2' by 4' (60.96 by 121.92cm) wide. To finish the throw, tie loose ends together and weave in excess yarn (f).

Windows Placemat and Gradient Block Coaster

The geometric design of this project pair makes for a perfect placemat and coaster set. Black, white, pink, and gray yarns work together wonderfully to add color and life to your table setting. Taking the pink yarn out of the coaster design still allows the two projects to match, while also giving your set some variety (because variety is the spice of life!).

KNOTTY LEVEL: 2
WORKING TIME: Placemat: 6 hours; coaster: 2–3 hours
FINISHED SIZE: Placemat: 12" x 18" (30.48 x 45.72cm); coaster: 4" x 4" (10.16 x 10.16cm)
CORDS: Placemat: bulky to super bulky weight yarn; coaster: cotton or synthetic worsted weight yarn

Windows Placemat

SUPPLIES

- 226' (68.88m) of assorted bulky weight yarn.
  Cut:
- (14) 4' (121.92cm) strands (horizontal cores)
- (14) 5' (152.40cm) strands (horizontal working strands)
- (20) 2' (60.96cm) strands (vertical cores)
- (20) 3' (91.44cm) strands (vertical working strands)
- Macramé board with T-pins (optional)

DIRECTIONS

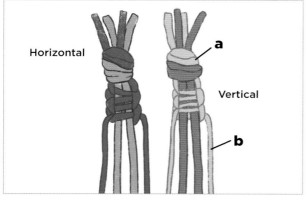

1 Group the strands in four, tie an overhand knot about 1" (2.54cm) from the end of each grouping (a), then tie two square knots (b). For arrangement, see the supplies list for the cut lengths.

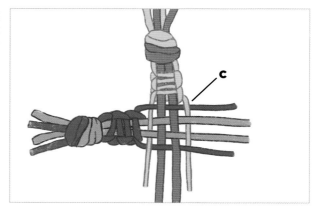

2 Beginning from the top left corner, weave the strands of one horizontal row and one vertical column (c).

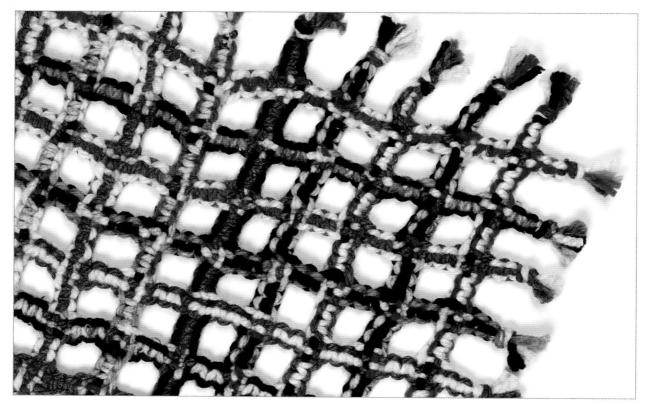

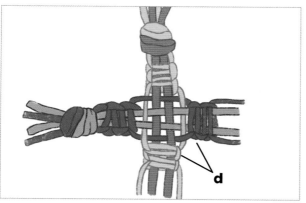

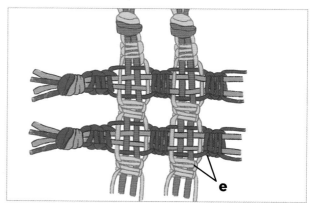

3 Tie two square knots on either side of the weave to secure (d).

4 Working down that first column, continue adding the next seven rows as from step 2. The weave should butt up against the previous square knots, then form two square knots on both sides of the weave to secure (e).

5 End the column with two square knots. Tie one overhand knot, then trim so that the fringe is about 1" (2.54cm) long.

6 Repeat steps 2 to 4 to set up the next nine columns.

Gradient Block Coaster

SUPPLIES

- (16) 18" (45.72cm) strands, for the core (4 each of 4 colors)
- (16) 12" (30.28cm) strands, for the working strands (4 each of 4 colors)
- Macramé board with T-pins (optional)

DIRECTIONS

Note: Follow the illustrations on pages 74 and 76.

1 Match the strands by color and group in units of four: short strands in the center to form the core. Tie an overhand knot about ½" (1.27cm) from the end of each grouping (a), then tie two square knots (b).

2 Arrange the colors from lightest to darkest: four across the top and four on the vertical axis. Beginning from the top left corner, weave the strands of two groups together (c). Tie two square knots on either side of the weave to secure (d).

3 Working down that first column, continue adding the next three rows as from step 2. The weave should butt up against the previous square knots, then form two square knots on both sides of the weave to secure (e).

4 End the column with two square knots. Tie one overhand knot, then trim so that the fringe is about ½" (1.27cm) long.

5 Repeat steps 2 to 4 to set up the next three columns.

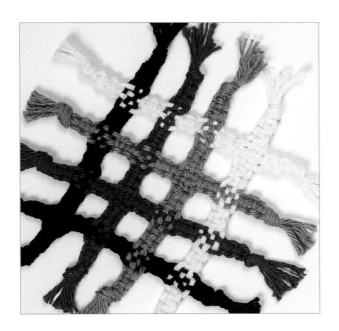

Three- or Four-Strand Base Design

Super chic, super modern, and easy. This plant hanger requires very little knotting; in fact, mastery of the overhand knot is the only knot required. This is a base, which means the design can be used as-is for a contemporary and quiet hanger, or later embellished as desired. Two embellishment patterns are in this book for variations on the square knot.

This pattern is shown for a three- and four-strand plant hanger, below. These patterns make a basic 36" (91.44cm)–long hanger to safely support a 4" to 8" (10.16 to 20.32cm) vessel. To adjust the length of the final hanger, double the length of the final desired size, then add 18" (45.72cm) for a three-strand design or 24" (60.96cm) for a four-strand design. The extra cord will compensate for the knots.

KNOTTY LEVEL: 1
WORKING TIME: 20 minutes
FINISHED SIZE: 36" (91.44cm) long
CORDS: 3–6mm–thick cotton, parachute cord, polypropylene, jute
SUPPLIES

Three-Strand Hanger
- (3) 7½'–8' (2.29–2.44m) lengths of desired cord

Four-Strand Hanger
- (4) 8'–8½' (2.44–2.59m) lengths of desired cord

DIRECTIONS

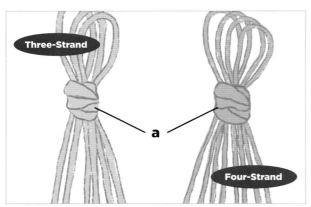

1 Find the center of the cotton cords and form a loop, and make one large overhand knot (a).

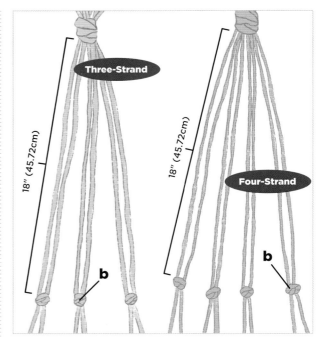

2 Pair off the strands and form overhand knots in each pairing, 18" (45.72cm) from the base of the large overhand knot (b).

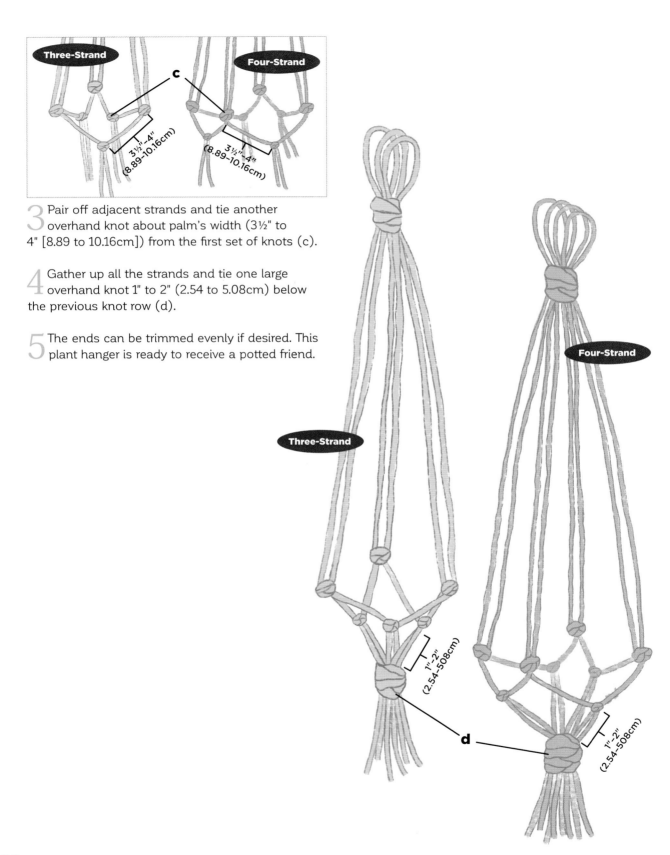

Three-Strand

Four-Strand

c

3½"–4"
(8.89–10.16cm)

3½"–4"
(8.89–10.16cm)

3 Pair off adjacent strands and tie another overhand knot about palm's width (3½" to 4" [8.89 to 10.16cm]) from the first set of knots (c).

4 Gather up all the strands and tie one large overhand knot 1" to 2" (2.54 to 5.08cm) below the previous knot row (d).

5 The ends can be trimmed evenly if desired. This plant hanger is ready to receive a potted friend.

Three-Strand

Four-Strand

1"–2"
(2.54–5.08cm)

1"–2"
(2.54–5.08cm)

d

Double Herb Holder

This simple, slim design adds a touch of visual interest. Need a quick hanging for a couple herbs? No problem! Using sturdy and dense cotton cord as a base, extra touches of color and texture are added to dress up the simple plant hanger base.

KNOTTY LEVEL: 1
WORKING TIME: 4 hours
FINISHED SIZE: 48" (1.22m) long
CORDS: Cotton, parachute cord, polypropylene, jute
SUPPLIES

- (4) 12' (3.66m) lengths of cotton rope (4mm)
- (12) 1' (30.48cm) lengths of colorful jute twine (2mm)
- (1) 7' (2.13m) length of colorful jute twine
- (2) 3' (91.44cm) lengths of colorful jute twine

DIRECTIONS

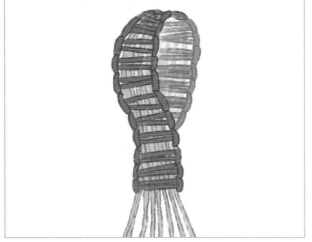

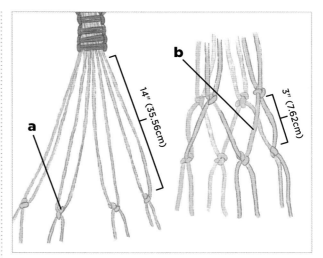

1 Find the center of the cotton cords and form a loop. Using the 7' (2.13m) strand of colorful jute, cover a 4" (10.16cm) section with a series of square knots, then rejoin to form a loop (see page 13).

2 Pair off the cotton strands and form a row of alternating half-hitches 14" (35.56cm) from the top loop (a).

3 Pair off the strands again with neighboring strands and form a second alternate half-hitch row about 3" (7.62cm) below the first (b).

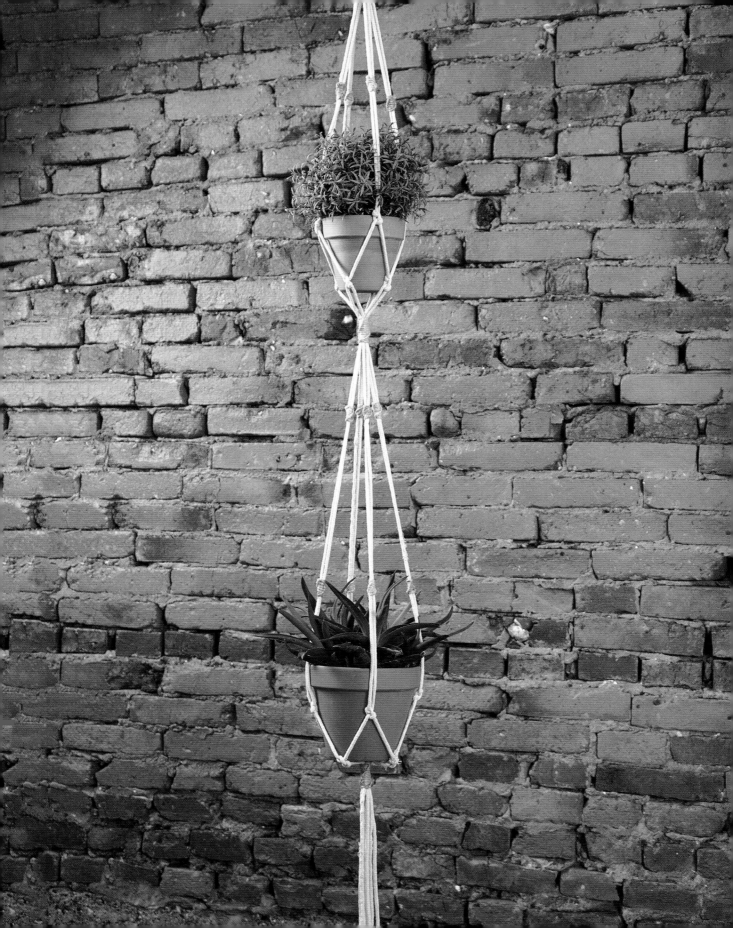

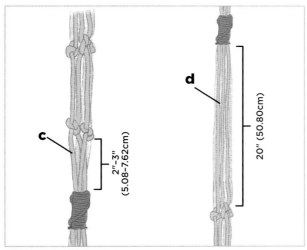

c

d

2"–3"
(5.08–7.62cm)

20" (50.80cm)

4 Gather up all the strands and wrap with a half-knot using one 3' (91.44cm) strand of colorful jute. Make sure you're wrapping it about 2" to 3" (5.08 to 7.62cm) below the second row of alternate half-hitch row (c).

5 Repeat steps 2 to 4 again, beginning 20" (50.80cm) below the wrap (d).

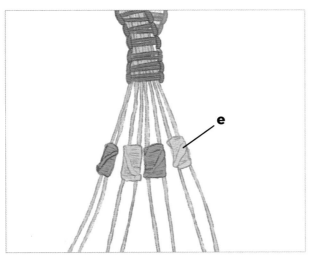

e

6 Embellish the hanger using the remaining strands of jute. Cover segments of the cotton with the jute, forming square or half-knots (e).

Switch Knot Embellishment Hanger

This pattern starts with a three-strand basic plant hanger design (see page 78). The switch knots in alternating colors will give your hanger something a little extra. I used a peachy pink on all three strands and changed between black, dark gray, and light gray for the other colors.

KNOTTY LEVEL: 1–2
WORKING TIME: 2–3 hours
FINISHED SIZE: 36" (91.44cm) long
CORDS: 3–6mm–thick cotton, parachute cord, polypropylene, jute, worsted weight
   yarns, strings, thread, ribbon
SUPPLIES
- **Three-Strand Hanger**
- (3) 7' 6" (228.60cm) lengths of desired cord (shown here using 4mm cotton twist)
- **Embellishments**
- (6) 12' (3.66m) lengths of 4 colors in cotton crochet yarn (three in color A,
   one in color B, one in color C, one in color D)
- Little bit of clear-dry craft glue

DIRECTIONS

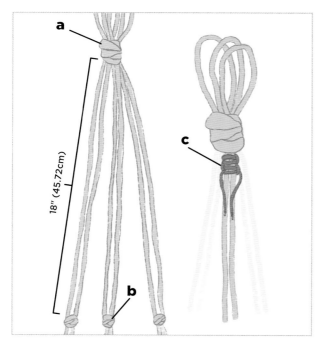

hanging strands, and form overhand knots in each pairing, 18" (45.72cm) from the base of the large overhand knot (b).

2 Starting from the base of the topknot, center the strands of color A and form two square knots (c).

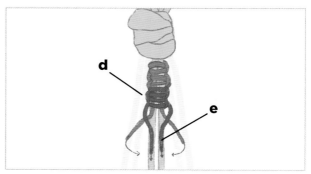

1 Gather and cut materials to form a three-strand plant hanger base. Find the center of the strands and tie one large overhand knot (a). Pair off the

3 Center the strands of color B just below the last square knot, and form two square knots around the full hanging strand (d). Tuck the strands of color B close to the hanger cords, and form two square knots around the grouping with color A (e).

4 Repeat this alternating pattern for 12" (30.48cm) (f). Repeat on the two other hanging strands, using one strand of color A and one strand of color C on the next strand. For the third, use one strand of color A and one of color D.

5 Follow the three-strand basic hanger directions (pages 78 and 80) for assembling the lower half (sling) portion of the hanger (g).

6 To finish, trim away excess yarn and add a dab of glue to secure the cut points.

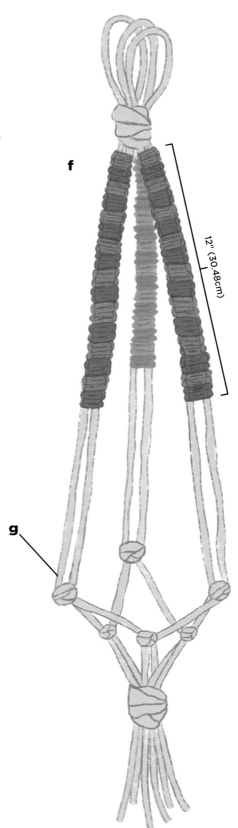

f

12" (30.48cm)

g

Wavy Embellishment Hanger

This pattern starts with a three-strand basic plant hanger design (see page 78). The knotted pattern used in this project adds a variation to the square knot. Instead of the blocked stripes you get in the Switch Knot Embellished Hanger (see page 84), the design I used in this project will give you a zigzagging pattern.

KNOTTY LEVEL: 1–2
WORKING TIME: 1.5 hours
FINISHED SIZE: 36" (91.44cm) long
CORDS: 3–6mm–thick cotton, parachute cord, polypropylene, jute, worsted weight yarns, strings, thread, ribbon
SUPPLIES
- (3) 7' 6" (228.60cm) lengths of desired cord (shown here using 4mm cotton twist)
- (6) 6' (182.88) lengths of 2 colors in cotton crochet yarn
- Little bit of clear-dry craft glue

DIRECTIONS

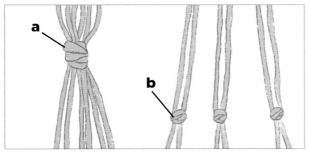

1 Begin with the formation of the three-strand plant hanger base. Find the center of the three large strands of cord and tie a large overhand knot (a). Tie two ends of contrasting cotton yarn together with an overhand or square knot (b).

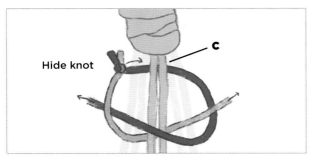

2 Center the knot of the cotton yarn behind two adjacent strands from the hanger, just below the topknot (c), and tie 12 half-knots.

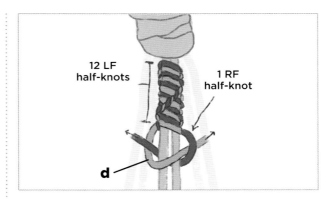

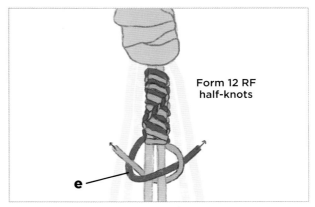

3 Next, tie one square knot (repeating the second half of the previous square knot) (d). Continue tying 12 half-knots so that they are rotating in the opposite direction (e).

4 Repeat step 3 again so that the half-knots flow in the other direction. Repeat until the yarn can no longer be knotted, or until the sinnet spans roughly 8" (20.32cm) in length (f). Continue this pattern on the two remaining hanging strands.

5 Trim away excess cord and add a dab of glue to the cut points. Follow the three-strand plant hanger base directions to finish the hanger.

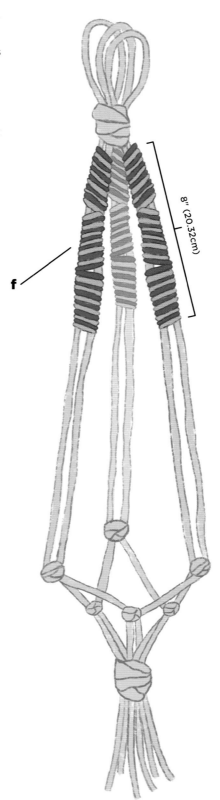

f

8" (20.32cm)

Air Plant Hanger

This is the home for an air plant that wants a bit of freedom and life. I found this sea urchin–style air plant holder at a local garden center. These are readily available online and through some local craft retailers. Real shells can be used as well. The ceramic holder offers the option to lightly paint it to match your home décor.

KNOTTY LEVEL: 1
WORKING TIME: 2–4 hours
FINISHED SIZE: 24" (60.96cm) long
CORDS: Yarns, cotton string or twine, jute, lightweight parachute cord, acrylic cord, polypropylene
SUPPLIES
- Metal ring
- (2) 8 yd. (7.32m) lengths of jute gauging about 1–2mm thickness (use thicker if the hole in the planter is particularly large) in two contrasting colors
- (1) 4' (1.22m) piece of jute
- Ceramic air plant holder or a small inverted terra-cotta pot
- Bit of clear-drying craft glue

DIRECTIONS

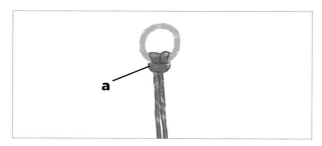

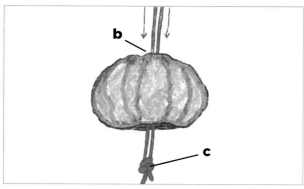

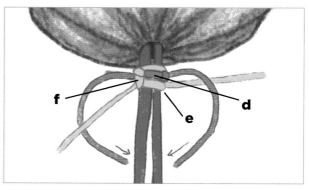

1. Use a lark's head knot to tie the 4' (121.92cm) piece of cord onto the ring (a), and thread the ends into the air plant holder (b). Tie them together with an overhand knot (c). Tug the knot into the planter. This will act as the core for the half knots.

2. Center and half-knot each of the two remaining cords into the core, just above the planter (d). Arrange the cords as shown (e) so that matching colors mirror one another on either side of the core, forming an "X."

3. With color A, form a half-knot (f). Move the strands out of the way and form a half-knot with color B.

4. Repeat the alternating half-knots until you reach the ring. For assistance, follow the Double Half-Knot instructions on page 21.

5. Trim the excess cord and apply a dab of clear-drying glue to the raw ends.

Braid-Braided Hanger

The simple design in this project makes it the perfect hanger for beginner macramé enthusiasts. It's a braided design made of braids. What could be easier?

I chose to go with a coastal palette, but you could choose any color combination you'd like to best suit your own décor. Jute comes in a variety of colors, so picking the ones you want to use might be your biggest challenge on this project!

KNOTTY LEVEL: 1–2
WORKING TIME: 2 hours
FINISHED SIZE: 36" (91.44cm) long
CORDS: Jute or cotton twines, no more than 2mm in thickness
SUPPLIES

- (6) 9' (2.74m) pieces of jute in color A
- (6) 9' (2.74m) pieces of jute in color B
- (6) 9' (2.74m) pieces of jute in color C
- (1) 7' (2.13m) piece of jute in color A

- (1) 3' (91.44cm) piece of jute in color A
- (3) Mini binder clips or paper clips or rubber bands
- Clear-drying tacky glue

DIRECTIONS

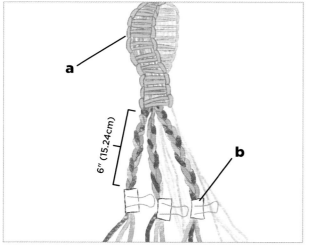

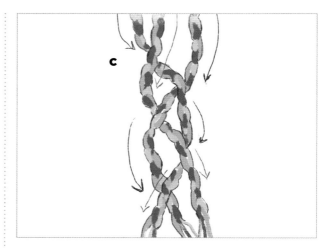

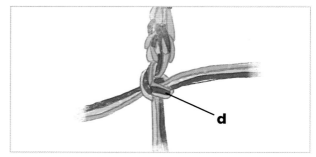

1 Gather and find the center for all the 9' (2.74m) strands of jute. Shift up about 2" (5.08cm) and center the 6' (1.83m) piece here. Follow the Plant Hanger Loop instructions on page 13 to complete the loop (a). Fold the sinnet in half when it reaches 4" (10.16cm) long. Continue to square knot around the bundle of cord until the working ends can no longer form knots (about 2" [5.08cm]).

2 Gather three strands, one of each color, and braid for 6" (15.24cm). Bind the ends to freely braid the next two groups (b).

3 Loosely braid these three braided strands together (c), then tie five half-knots to secure, using the center braid as an anchor (d).

4 Repeat step 3 for two more segments. The final length of this strand will be roughly 20" (50.80cm) long.

5 Repeat steps 2 to 4 until there are four large hanging braids.

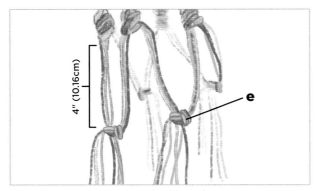

6 Drop down about 4" (10.16cm) below the half-knots and form a row of square knots with adjacent segments, two parts from the left strand and one from the right. Working clockwise around the hanger, make three more square knots to complete this row (e).

7 Form one more row of alternating square knots about 3" (7.62cm) below the previous row (f).

8 Gather the strands at the bottom of the hanger and center the 3' (91.44cm) strands of jute about 1" to 2" (2.54 to 5.08cm) below the last row of overhand knots. Form a series of square knots (g).

9 Snip away excess jute from the square knots, and apply a dab of glue to the cut points to prevent unraveling.

Josephine Twist Hanger

This plant hanger features a lovely blend of braiding and decorative knotting. You can create very clean lines with a four-strand braid. When paired with a pretty Josephine knot, it's a great way to add a little pizazz to your hanger's strands.

KNOTTY LEVEL: 2
WORKING TIME: 2–3 hours
FINISHED SIZES: 36" (91.44cm) long
CORDS: 3–4mm cords, cotton braid or twist, polypropylene
SUPPLIES

- (4) 10' (3.05m) pieces of 4mm polypropylene in color A
- (4) 10' (3.05m) pieces of 4mm polypropylene in color B
- (2) 18" (45.72cm) pieces of 4mm polypropylene in either color
- Metal ring
- Lighter (optional)

DIRECTIONS

1 Gather and find the center for all the 12' (3.66m) strands of cord and center onto the metal ring. Use one 18" (45.72cm) strand of cord and wrap the gathered cord at the base of the ring to secure (a). Group the cords into four groups of four strands, providing two strands of each color in each group.

2 Form 3" (7.62cm) of the four-strand braid (b), then form one Josephine knot (c). Knot 8" (20.32cm) of the four-strand braid, form a Josephine knot (d), form 10" (25.40cm) of four-strand braid, then finish with a Josephine knot.

3 Repeat the pattern from step 2 across the three remaining sections of cord.

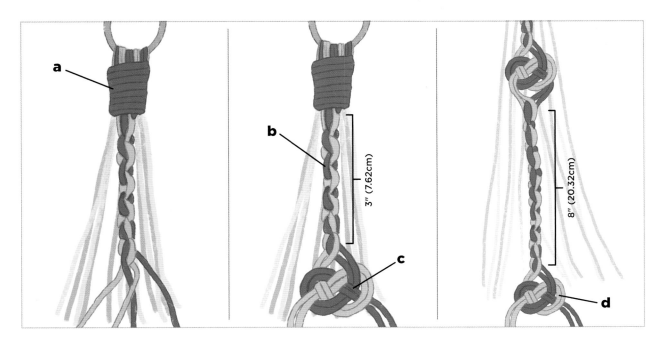

4 To form the plant hanger sling, drop down about 3" (7.62cm) from the final Josephine knot and form a row of alternating square knots. Drop down about 2" (5.08cm) to form another alternate row of square knots, and then one more row of alternate square knots another 1" (2.54cm) below.

5 To finish the hanger, gather all the cords just below the final row of square knots and wrap with the remaining 18" (45.72cm) strand of cord. Trim the ends to the desired length. When using polypropylene, the tips of the cord can be melted with a lighter to prevent fray (optional).

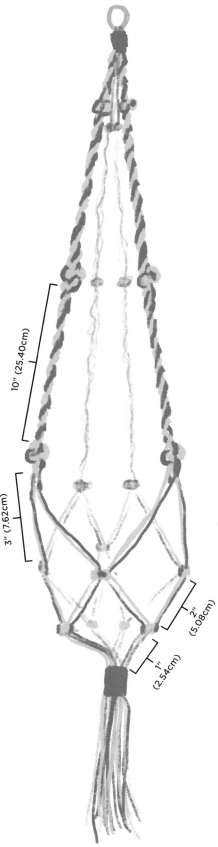

10" (25.40cm)

3" (7.62cm)

2" (5.08cm)

1" (2.54cm)

Lacy Ribbon Hanger

The ribbon selected for this project is a lovely cream lace that lends a little vintage flair to this plant hanger. A boldly printed ribbon would suit this project, as well, as it will be subdued by the rickrack edging. This is a petite plant holder that can support an 8 oz. to 12 oz. (226.80 to 340.19g) plant safely.

KNOTTY LEVEL: 2
WORKING TIME: 4 hours
FINISHED SIZE: 30" (76.20cm) long
CORDS: Ribbon, yarns, cotton string or twine, jute, lightweight parachute cord, acrylic cord, polypropylene
SUPPLIES

- (2) 3' (91.44cm) lengths of ⅝"–1" (1.59–2.54cm) ribbon
- (8) 16' (4.88m) lengths of cotton crochet yarn
- (2) 2' (60.96cm) pieces of cotton crochet yarn
- (1) Metal ring
- 4"–6" (10.16–15.24cm) plant holder
- Metal hook (optional)
- Bit of clear-drying craft glue

DIRECTIONS

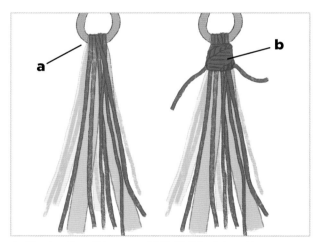

1 Center the ribbon and 16' (4.88m) lengths of yarn onto the metal ring (a). Using one 2' (60.96cm) length of yarn, wrap or tie a series of half-knots around the hanging strands just below the ring (b).

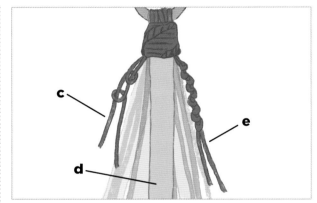

2 Group the cords into three segments that consist of two pieces of yarn knotted with 10 half-hitches (c), one length of ribbon center (d), and two more pieces of yarn knotted with 10 half-hitches (e).

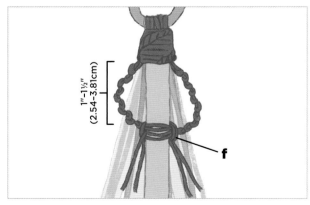

3 Form a square around the piece of ribbon, using two strands of yarn at a time. Tie one square knot around the ribbon (f). There should be a 1" to 1½" (2.54 to 3.81cm) gap between each square knot.

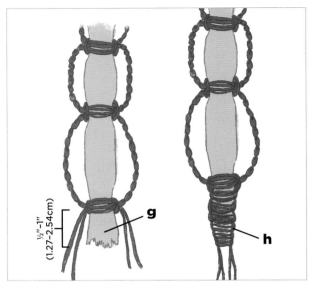

½"–1"
(1.27–2.54cm)

g

h

4 Repeat step 3 about ½" to 1" (1.27 to 2.54cm) or so from the end of the ribbon (g). From there, tie square knots around the ribbon to the end (h). If the end of the ribbon is frayed, slip the yarns so that there are two center core strands and form three to five square knots until it's secure. Repeat this process on the three remaining hanging segments.

5 Begin forming the pot-holder sling about 2½" to 3" (6.35 to 7.62cm) below the finished hanging cords (i). Use a square knot on the adjacent strands. On the next row, settle the alternate square knots 1½" to 2" (3.81 to 5.08cm) from the previous row. Finish by gathering up all the hanging strands and tying one large overhand knot just below the second row (j). Trim the ends to the desired length.

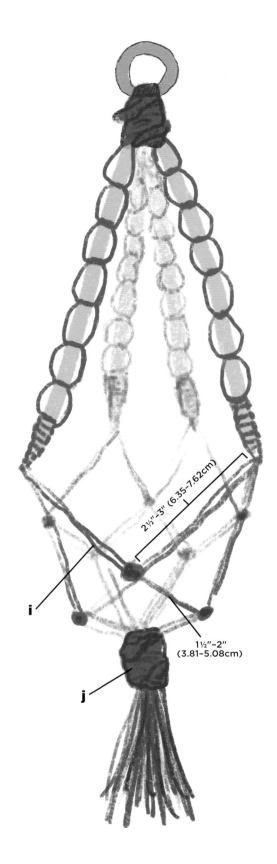

2½"–3" (6.35–7.62cm)

i

1½"–2"
(3.81–5.08cm)

j

Raindrop Hanger

This airy little number is recommended for dangling light or delicate planters. The alternating half-hitch used in suspension allows for stretching and relaxing with gravity. The decorative raindrops add a touch of rustic charm, melding the planter with the plant. Partially inspired by jade and string of pearl succulents.

KNOTTY LEVEL: 2
WORKING TIME: 2 hours
FINISHED SIZES: 36" (91.44cm) long
CORDS: 1.5–2mm cotton string or twine, jute, lightweight parachute cord, acrylic cord, or 2mm polypropylene
SUPPLIES
- Metal ring
- (4) 16' (4.88m) lengths of jute gauging about 1.5–2mm thickness
- Glass or light ceramic plant holder up to 8" (20.32cm) wide
- Bit of clear-drying craft glue

DIRECTIONS

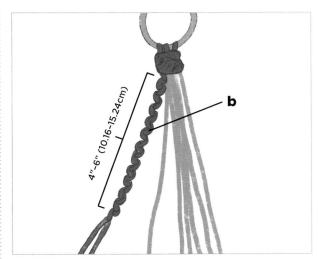

1 Center the four strands of cord onto the metal ring and tie one large overhand knot, butting against the base of the ring (a).

2 Pair off the strands and tie a 4" to 6" (10.16 to 15.24cm) sinnet of alternating half-hitches (about 24 to 40 alternating half-hitches) (b).

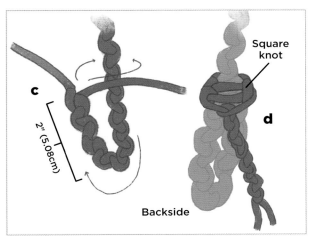

Square knot

c

2" (5.08cm)

Backside

d

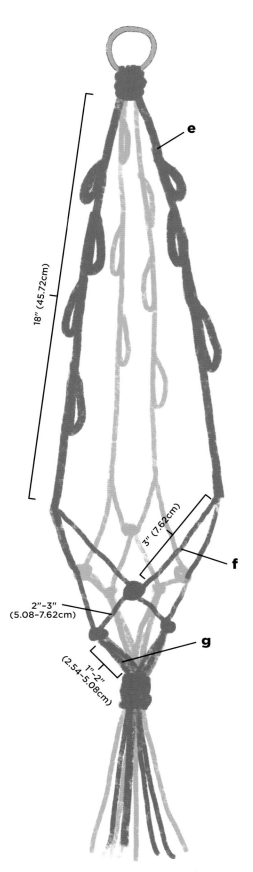

18" (45.72cm)

e

3" (7.62cm)

f

2"–3"
(5.08-7.62cm)

g

1"-2"
(2.54-5.08cm)

3 Fold up about 2" (5.08cm) (c) and form a square knot over the sinnet to secure the teardrop shape (d). Continue the sinnet strand for another 4" to 6" (10.16 to 15.24cm). Make 3 or 4 "raindrops" as desired.

4 Keep applying the teardrop pattern until the length of the sinnet is roughly 18" (45.72cm) (e). Repeat the process along the three remaining pairs of cord. Staggering the "raindrop" positions from strand-to-strand will make the hanger appear organic.

5 Form the sling about 3" (7.62cm) below the half-hitch sinnets. Combine one strand from each adjacent hanging string with either an alternating half-hitch (as used in the photographed project) or an overhand knot (f). Form the next (alternate) row 2" to 3" (5.08 to 7.62cm) below, and finish by gathering all the strands at the base and tying one large overhand knot 1" to 2" (2.54 to 5.08cm) from the previous row (g).

6 Trim the hanging fringe to the desired length. Clear-drying glue can be applied to the tips of the fringe to prevent fray.

Ribbon Globe Hanger

This project best suits a lightweight air plant, succulent, or cactus. The knot tying on its own would make for a pretty little chain. The addition of the ribbon brightens the volume of the plant hanger presence, so that it doesn't blend into its surroundings. For an alternative, see the Lacy Ribbon Hanger on page 98 for suspending a small traditional planter.

KNOTTY LEVEL: 1–2
WORKING TIME: 2 hours
FINISHED SIZE: 30" (76.20cm) long
CORDS: Ribbon, yarns, cotton string or twine, jute, lightweight parachute cord, acrylic cord, polypropylene
SUPPLIES

- (1) 6' (182.88cm) length of 2"–3" (5.08–7.62cm) ribbon
- (2) 16' (4.88cm) lengths of jute, with gauge thickness of about 1–2mm in two contrasting colors (use thicker strands if the planter hole is large)
- Glass globe succulent hanger
- Metal hook (optional)
- Bit of clear-drying craft glue

DIRECTIONS

1 Tie a lark's head knot (or simply center and loop the ribbon) onto the container, then tie the ends together with an overhand knot (a). If squeamish about potentially breaking the container as knots are installed, loop the ribbon into a metal hook (optional) that can be later attached to the hanger.

2 Center the two strands of jute at the base of the hanger, and tie an overhand knot (b).

3 Form a series of ten alternating half-hitches with each of the two cord pairings (c). Tie one square knot around the ribbon (d).

4 Repeat step three to the top of the hanger. Allow a couple inches (several centimeters) at the top for hanging (e). Finish with two square knots at the top of the hanger, then trim excess jute and add a dab of glue to the cut points to secure.

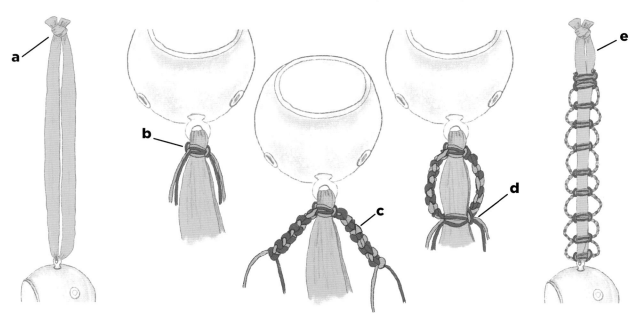

Stitched Plant Hanger

This plant hanger can really be made from any material. I used 2mm jute to make the small and one of the larger hangers, and 4mm polypropylene braid to make a large hanger as well. Some of the jute was hand-painted to facilitate with the rustic look. What's extra special about this project is that it only requires one knot to complete the whole project.

KNOTTY LEVEL: 1
WORKING TIME: 1–2 hours
FINISHED SIZES: Small, about 18" (45.72cm) long; large, about 36" (91.44cm) long
CORDS: 4–6mm cords (braided or twisted), jute, cotton, polypropylene, or nylon
SUPPLIES

Small Hanger:
- Metal or wooden ring
- (2) 4' (121.92cm) pieces of neutral cord A
- (4) 7' (213.36cm) pieces of neutral cord A
- (2) 4' (121.92cm) pieces of colorful cord B
- (2) 2' (60.96cm) pieces of colorful cord B

Large Hanger:
- Metal or wooden ring
- (2) 8' (243.84cm) pieces of neutral cord A
- (4) 14' (426.72cm) pieces of neutral cord A
- (2) 8' (243.84cm) pieces of colorful cord B
- (2) 2' (60.96cm) pieces of colorful cord B

DIRECTIONS

1 Set the two 2' (60.96cm) pieces of cord aside. Center the remaining pieces of cord onto the ring. It may be easiest to center the long strands first, then center the shorter pieces.

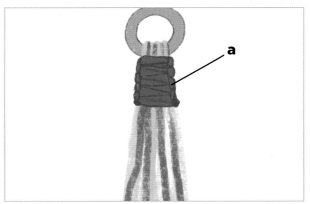

2 Center one of the 2' (60.96cm) pieces of cord directly under the ring and tie a square knot around the bundle (a). This will secure the hanging pieces in place. Square knot until you run out of cord. Snip away any excess flyaway strands.

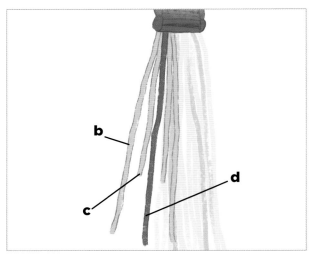

3 Separate and arrange the first hanging line: two long neutral strands on the outside (b), two shorter neutral strands next (c), and one long color strand in the center (d).

Small Hanger

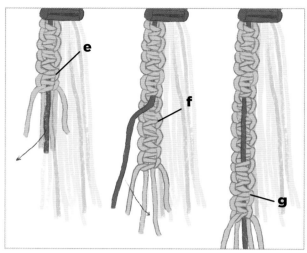

4 Tie five square knots with the long outer strands (e). Bring the colorful strand forward, and form three more square knots with the neutral cord (f). Next, slide the colorful cord back into the center and form five more square knots on top of it (g). Repeat this step one more time for the small hanger and four more times to make a long hanger.

5 Repeat steps 3 and 4 on the remaining sections.

6 Once you have the four complete hanging strands, form the basket sling. On a small hanger, form two rows of alternating square knots about 3" (7.62cm) apart (h). For the large hanger, form two rows of alternating square knots about 5" (12.70cm) apart (i).

7 Gather all the cords about an inch or two (several centimeters) below the last row of knots. Center the last strand of colorful cord and form another series of square knots. Snip away the excess.

8 Trim the hanger fringe to the length you desire.

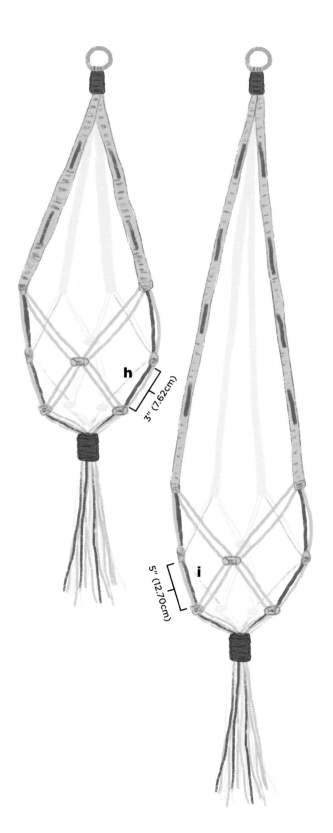

Twinkle Plant Hanger

Sparkles and fringe-free? Yep! This little hanger is designed to be seen day or night. It casts the illusion of falling stars. This hanger is best to be paired with artificial plants for a no-mess access to the on/off switch. While the weight is bared by the jute alone, the string of lights are very light, so keep the plant profile small and light; plants under 2 lbs. (0.91kg) and 6" (15.24cm) are ideal. This project only utilizes half-knots and overhand knots, but what makes it challenging is the balancing act of keeping the light strands level as the knots are installed.

KNOTTY LEVEL: 3
WORKING TIME: 3 hours
FINISHED SIZE: 36" (91.44cm) long
CORDS: 2mm cords, cotton braid or twist, jute, nylon, polypropylene, or worsted weight yarn in cotton or acrylic
SUPPLIES

- Metal or wooden ring
- (4) 8' (2.44cm) pieces of neutral cord A
- (4) 8' (2.44cm) pieces of neutral cord B
- (2) Battery-powered strings of lights (10' [3.05m] string) plus batteries
- 6" (15.24cm) planter with center drainage hole
- Tape
- Clear-drying glue

DIRECTIONS

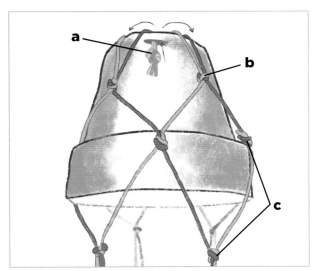

1 Gather all the jute and pass it up through the drainage hole of the planter, then tie one large overhand knot to keep it from escaping through the bottom of the pot (a).

2 Keeping the planter upside down, pair off the jute strands to form the netting. Form a row of overhand knots by the edge of the planter base (b).

Proceed to re-pair off the jute to form two additional rows of alternate overhand knots (c).

> **TIP:** Gather up all the jute and temporarily tie a large overhand knot to keep the net from sliding when the pot is turned upright.

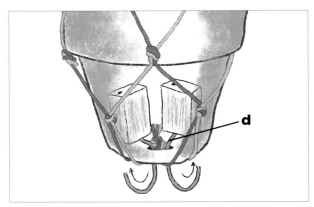

3 Turn the planter right side up and feed the two strings of lights out through the drainage hole from the inside of the planter (d).

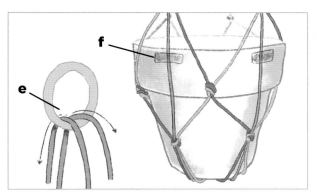

light strand (h). Allow the last 6" to 8" (15.24 to 20.32cm) at the top to remain knot free.

7 Once all the strands are covered, pass the jute through the metal ring and tie a chunky half-knot sinnet around the hanging to secure (i). Tie until the chunky square knot is about 3" (7.62cm) long.

8 Finish by trimming away the excess jute and apply a bit of glue to the unfinished ends to keep it secure. Remove all the tape. The wire lights that were taped to the pot can be folded up and twisted into the hanger. The area above the lip of the pot is the only portion that should be lit; the netting around the pot should not contain any lights. Add the plant and hang when the plant hanger is fully cured.

4 Thread the light strands through the metal ring, finding the centers (e), and then tape the lights in place around the planter (f). Arrange the strands so that the two unlit, plastic-covered parts of the strands are opposite one another on the pot, and the two lit portions of the strands are also opposite one another.

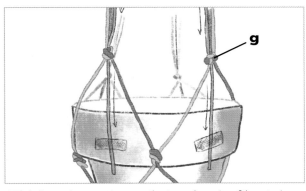

5 Adjust the netting so that each pair of knots in the jute string will align with a strand of lights. Tie ten half-knots around the light strands, starting just above the lip of the pot (g).

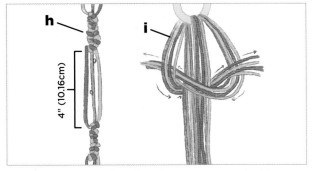

6 It may help to lay the planter on its side. Every 4" (10.16cm), knot ten half-knots along each

Boho Owl

In the 1970s, macramé owls were a huge trend, so I decided to bring it back with this cute project that's perfect for those that have strands of scrap ribbon or cord lying around. This is a simple yet bold solution to dealing with craft scraps and putting them on display for all to see.

KNOTTY LEVEL: 1
WORKING TIME: 30–60 minutes
FINISHED SIZES: 18"–24" (45.72–60.96cm) long
CORDS: Fabric strips, ribbon, yarn, cotton cord
SUPPLIES

- (12–16) 5' (1.52m) strands of assorted cord
- (2) 15mm plastic animal eyes with backs

DIRECTIONS

1 Gather cords into two groups and tie together with large overhand knots on one end (a).

2 Spit the groups into three chunky sections and braid together (b). Secure the end with another large overhand knot.

3 Tie two large Josephine knots with the two braided segments (c).

4 Untie the overhand knots. Gather the cords at the bottom and wrap a scrap piece of cord to tether the strands together (d). To form the owl horns (for hanging), fold down the loose segments and knot off (e).

5 Add the eyes (f). Mount the eyes in the upper Josephine knot. Wiggle eyes can be substituted and glued to the form if there are no flat segments to secure the eye posts.

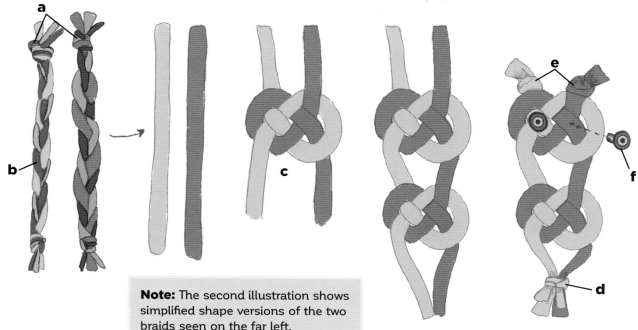

Note: The second illustration shows simplified shape versions of the two braids seen on the far left.

Bright Banners (Three Ways)

Perfect for a party—but even better as a permanent part of your home's décor—these colorful banners will complement any space. Make all three for a fun way to add a little color to your life. Though they look great as is, you could embellish the finished banners by embroidering letters, numbers, or a pretty design with a large-eyed needle and contrasting yarn.

KNOTTY LEVEL: 1
WORKING TIME: 4–6 hours per banner string
FINISHED SIZE: 10' wide x 5"–6" tall (304.80 x 12.7–15.24cm)
CORDS: Yarns, braided or twisted cotton string or twine, fabric strips, polypropylene, parachute cord (any weight)

Pennant Flags

SUPPLIES

- (80) 2' foot strands of cotton yarn
- (1) 10' (304.80cm) strand of cotton yarn
- Crochet hook (optional)

TIP: Recommended worsted or medium weight cord, but this project will work on any scale. Add 12" (30.48cm) to the cut cords when using bulky or dense cords.

DIRECTIONS

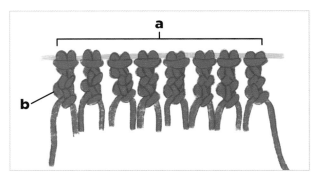

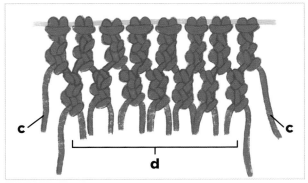

1 Each flag requires eight strands of yarn. Using the 10' (3.05m) strand of cotton yarn as a mounting cord, make lark's head knots with the eight strands of cotton yarn (a). There will now be sixteen hanging strands.

2 Pair off the hanging strands and form four alternating half-hitches across the full row. There will be eight knotted strands on this row (b).

3 For row 2, drop the first and last strands (c). Pair off the adjacent strands and form four alternating half-hitches on each. There will be six knotted hanging strands on this row (d).

TIP: This is a small and portable project. Use a safety pin to clip each flag to your pant leg or skirt to keep it steady.

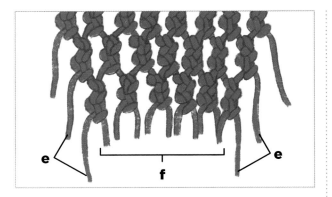

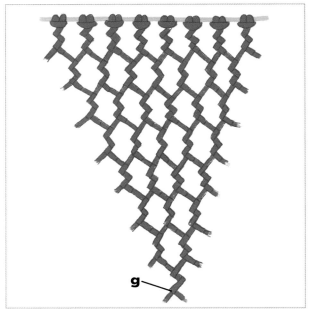

4 In rows 3 to 5, drop the first and last strands (e) and repeat the alternate half-hitch technique from the previous rows (f). The rows will decrease to four, two, and one knot on each row (g).

5 Trim fringe as desired. Ends can be tucked into the back and trim for a fringe-free look.

6 Repeat steps 1 to 5 for additional flags (this pattern calls for a total of ten pennant flags).

Banner Flags

SUPPLIES

- (60) 2' (60.96cm) strands of cotton yarn
- (20) 1' (30.48cm) strands of cotton yarn
- (1) 10' (3.05m) strand of cotton yarn

DIRECTIONS

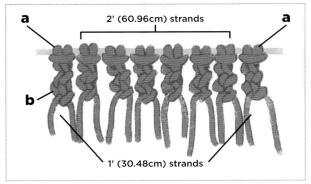

1 Each flag requires six 2' (60.96cm) and two 1' (30.48cm) strands of yarn. Using the 10' (3.05m) strand of cotton yarn as a mounting cord, make lark's head knots with the eight strands of cotton yarn; keep the two 1' (30.48cm) strands on the outside (a). There will now be sixteen hanging strands.

2 Form four alternating half-knots in the first row. There will be eight completed knots on this row (b).

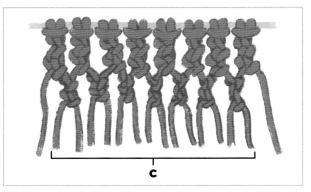

3 Drop the first and last stands on this row. Pair off the hanging strands and form four alternating half-hitches with each pairing. There will be seven knots on this row (c).

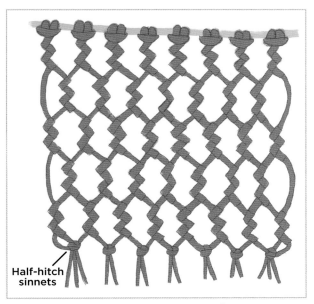

Half-hitch sinnets

4 Continue this decreasing method (dropping two strands from a row) for six more rows. The final row will have only one alternate half-hitch sinnet.

5 Trim fringe as desired. Ends can be tucked into the back, and trim for a fringe-free look.

6 Repeat steps 1 to 5 for additional flags (this pattern calls for a total of ten).

Fish Tail Flags

SUPPLIES

- (80) 2' (60.96cm) strands of cotton yarn
- (1) 10' (304.80cm) strand of cotton yarn
- Crochet hook (optional)

DIRECTIONS

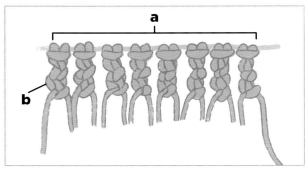

1 Each flag requires eight strands of yarn. Using the 10' (3.05m) strand of cotton yarn as a mounting cord, make lark's head knots with the eight strands of cotton yarn (a). There will now be sixteen hanging strands.

2 Form four alternating half-hitch knots in the first row. There will be eight completed knots on this row (b).

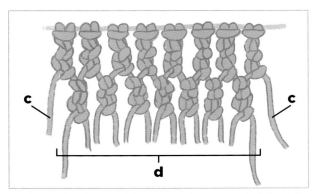

3 Drop the first and last strands on row 2 (c) and form a row of alternating half-hitch knots. There will be seven knots on this row (d).

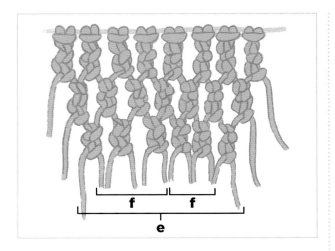

6 Trim fringe as desired, or use a crochet hook to weave the cords into the backside of the flag.

7 Repeat steps 1 to 6 for additional flags (this pattern calls for a total of ten).

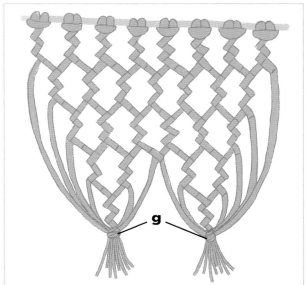

4 On row 3, form six sets of four alternating half-hitches (e).

5 For rows 4 and 5, decrease the two segments separately (f). Each part will decrease to two knots, and then one knot (g).

Cotton Candy Dream Catcher

Dreamy and romantic, this dream catcher sings for sweet dreams and pleasant mornings. The ribbons used around the perimeter of the ring are quite bulky; in fact, the bulkier the better! The mixture of the textures and volumes makes a luscious concoction for the eyes. The little pops of color stuck in the webbing emulates the captured dreams turned to sugar.

KNOTTY LEVEL: 2
WORKING TIME: 8–10 hours
FINISHED SIZE: 15" round x 25" long (38.10 x 63.50cm)
CORDS: Yarns, cotton string or twine, jute string, ribbon
SUPPLIES

- 12"–15" (30.48–38.10cm) metal ring
  (**NOTE:** Use the second lampshade ring from the Tutu Chandelier project on page 59)
- (3) 2 yd. (1.83m) lengths of assorted ribbon
- 30'–36' (9.14–10.97cm) length of cotton yarn or 1mm hemp
- About 100 yd. (91.44m) of cotton yarn in assorted (coordinating) colors
- Macramé brush (optional)
- Tape

DIRECTIONS

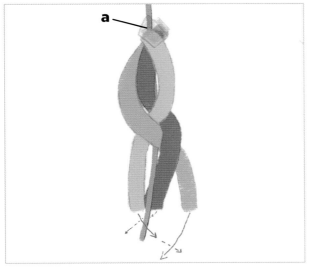

1 Loosely tape one end of the three ribbons to the metal ring (a). Braid around the ring until you run out of ribbon.

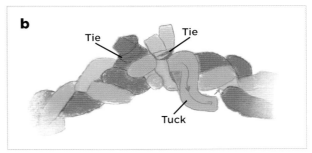

2 Once you've circled back to the beginning, release the tape. Tuck, weave, and tie the ends concealing the beginning/end (b).

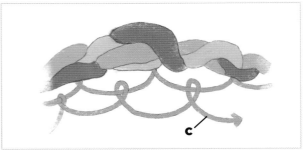

3 Tie one end of the cotton cord to the metal ring and hitch a web on the inside of the ring (c). I cut this into 12' to 15' (3.66 to 4.57m) sections to make this process easier. I would add more cord by just tying the new and old ends together with an overhand knot. Once you find the center, tie off and trim away the excess.

4 To form feathers, cut a length of yarn 18" to 24" (45.72 to 60.96cm) long and tie a series of lark's head knots on the cord at the base of the dream catcher (d). Tie an overhand knot at the end of the cord.

5 Cut 12" (30.48cm) pieces from the same cord: 40 to 50 pieces for smaller feathers, and about 70 to 80 for the larger feathers. Find the center of two pieces and use a reef knot to tie them to the hanging strand (see page 14 for more detailed instructions). Repeat this until the feather achieves the fullness to your liking (e).

OPTIONAL: Brush out the feathers to make them a bit puffier.

6 Add as many feathers as you'd like. To embellish further, tie little trimmings from the cord (2" to 3" [5.08 to 7.62cm] pieces) to random spots in the webbing to symbolize caught dreams.

Feathered Hanging

Feather bomb! This simple hanging takes on two layers: the back layer of kite tail–like fabric "feathers" trickle color into the foreground neutral-toned cotton yarn feathers. Like the Patch Scrap Mat (see page 65), this is an excellent way to use up scraps from your fabric stash.

KNOTTY LEVEL: 1–2
WORKING TIME: 2 hours
FINISHED SIZE: 18" x 18" (45.72 x 45.72cm)
CORDS: Cotton string, cotton cord, fabric strips, or ribbon
SUPPLIES

- (6) 1" x 14"–18" (2.54 x 35.56–45.72cm) lengths of fabric (or ribbon)
- (120) 1" (2.54cm)–wide strips of fabric (or ribbon), cut 5"–7" (12.70–17.78cm) long
- (3) 3' (91.44cm) pieces of cotton cord
- (30) 8" (20.32cm) pieces of cotton cord
- (48) 6" (15.24cm) pieces of cotton cord
- (1) 2' (60.96cm) length of 2–3mm cotton cord (for hanging)
- 18" (45.72cm) branch (or a dowel rod)
- Macramé brush

DIRECTIONS

1 Tie the 2" (60.96cm) length of jute to both ends of the branch for hanging.

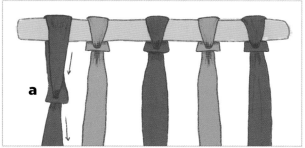

2 Cut small holes into one end of each of the long strips of fabric and tie lark's head knots across the branch (a). Knot the tip of the fabric strips.

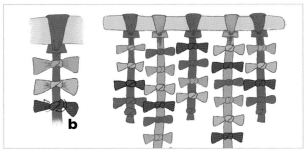

3 To fill the feathers, tie each small strip of fabric to the long strand using half-knots (b). Fill each feather to the desired fullness, which should take 15 to 20 strips. Optional: Cut little slits into the fabric to add more feathering.

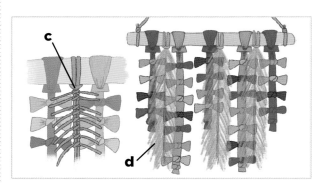

4 Form the front feathers (see page 14) by folding the 3' (91.44cm) lengths of cord in half and tie lark's head knots to the branch (c). Tie an overhand knot into the end. Tie ten 8" (20.32cm) segments of cotton to the top portion of the feather with a half-knot. Tie sixteen 6" (15.24cm) pieces into the lower half of the feather. Unravel feather twists and fluff to make a fuller appearance (d).

Mock Stockinette Tapestry

This tapestry is super simple to produce, and it makes for a great ambitious project for a novice knotter. The pattern requires only the use of an overhand knot and a half-hitch. The ultra-plushy yarn will bring softness to any bedroom.

KNOTTY LEVEL: 1–2
WORKING TIME: 8–12 hours
FINISHED SIZE: Approximately 4' x 3' (121.92 x 91.44cm)
CORDS: Ultra bulky acrylic weight yarns
SUPPLIES

- 600' (274.32m) ultra thick acrylic yarn (⅝"–¾" [1.59–1.91cm] round):
  50 strands cut to 12' (3.66m) each (42 pieces in color A; 8 pieces in color B)
- Large corkboard
- (12+) T-pins

DIRECTIONS

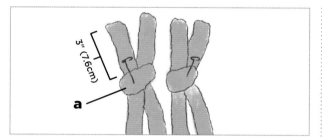

1 Pair off the cords and tie one large overhand knot 3" (7.62cm) from one end (a). Tack the cords up onto a wall or board (recommended) and arrange the strands as shown (b).

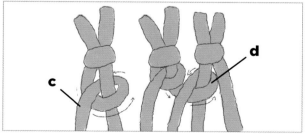

2 Starting from the left, half-hitch the left strand to the right (c). Take the right strand and half-hitch to the next cord to the right (d). Carry on to the end of the row.

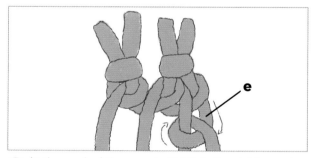

3 At the end of the row, half-hitch the right-most strand to the left (e). Continue this pattern to the end of the row.

4 Repeat steps 2 to 3 until the tapestry measures 3' (91.44cm), or until the shortest strand is roughly 6" (15.24cm) long.

5 Along the bottom, pair off the cords and tie an overhand knot so it butts up to the edge. Trim the fringe to 3" (7.62cm) long.

Psst!
Want to turn this into a
4' x 5' (1.22 x 1.52m)
throw? Cut the yarn into
18' (5.49m) lengths. This
blanket will require
900' (274.32m)
of yarn.

Kite Tail Curtain

Create a boho version of those beaded curtains. This project makes a beautiful fabric stash disappear in plain sight. It's easy to customize the scale of this curtain to fit any doorway or window. Measure the height of the curtain space, then double that number for the cord length; the number of strands equals the width in inches. This project is quiet easy, but it makes a bold statement.

KNOTTY LEVEL: 1–2
WORKING TIME: 12–24 hours (weekend project)
FINISHED SIZE: 3' wide x 6' tall (91.44 x 182.88cm)
CORDS: Heavy yarns, braided or twisted cotton string or twine, fabric strips
SUPPLIES

- (36) 13' (3.96m) strands of cotton cord
- Spring-loaded drapery that fits a doorway or window (or substitute with 3½' [1.07m] strand of cotton cord with tacks for mounting)
- 216 pieces of fabric clippings (about ¼" [0.64cm]–wide strips cut into 8"–10" [20.32–25.40cm] lengths)
- 216' (65.84m) cotton crochet yarn (multiple colors cut into 12" [30.48cm] lengths)

DIRECTIONS

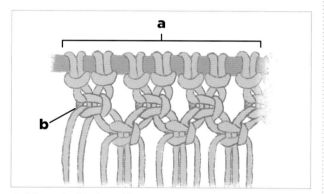

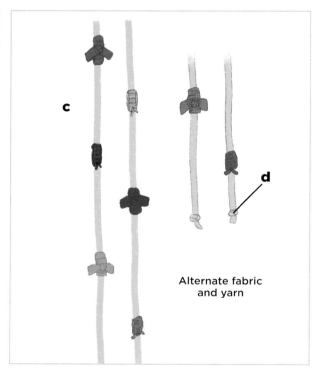

Alternate fabric and yarn

1 Use a lark's head knot to tie the 36 strands of cotton cord onto the drapery rod (a). There will be 72 hanging strands.

2 Form one row of square knots, followed by one row of alternating square knots (b). This will help secure the curtain and distribute the hanging strands.

3 Along each strand, use a square knot to tie three fabric strips and three pieces of yarn onto the lengths of cord (c). Evenly distribute the cotton yarn and fabric clippings, alternating the cotton yarn and fabric pieces.

4 Tie an overhand knot at the bottom of each strand to prevent fray and help weigh down the ends (d).

5 Hang as desired.

Giant Dreams

Dreamy colors and flowing fabric were used to make this beautiful dream catcher. I loved the idea of incorporating an embroidery hoop into the design, and when paired with pretty lace, the two provided the perfect vintage flair. Since the outer ring is made with a Hula Hoop, this massive dream catcher will be a breeze to hang.

KNOTTY LEVEL: 1
WORKING TIME: 3–6 hours
FINISHED SIZE: 24" (60.96cm) round
CORDS: Mixed cord, ribbon, cotton yarn, cotton rope, jute rope, twine, burlap
SUPPLIES

- (1) 24" (60.96cm) Hula-Hoop
- (1) 12" (30.48cm) embroidery hoop
- (1) 14" x 14" (35.56 x 35.56cm) piece of lace, or a large doily
- (1) 12' (3.66m) strand of cotton yarn in neutral color
- Large-eye needle (optional)
- (1) 15' (4.57m) length of 4" (10.16cm) burlap ribbon
- Ribbon of mixed textures and colors (shown: 4" [10.16cm] burlap ribbon, cotton thread, assorted lacy ribbons, and sheer satin ribbons)
- Clear-drying craft glue (optional)

DIRECTIONS

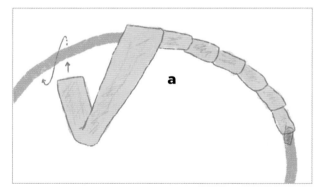

1 Strip the Hula-Hoop down to the bare bones. Tape one end of the burlap ribbon to the Hula-Hoop and begin wrapping it around (a). If necessary, glue the ends together to keep the wrapped burlap stable (b).

2 Tie the ends of two colorful ribbons together with an overhand knot, and center the knot on the underside of the Hula-Hoop (c). Form loose half-knots (spaced about 1½" [3.81cm] apart) around the Hula-Hoop to cover (d). Once circled back to the beginning, discreetly weave the ends into the circle.

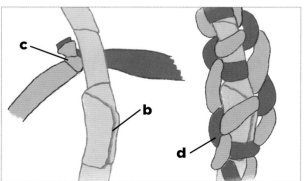

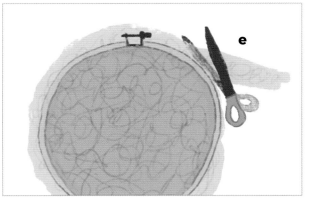

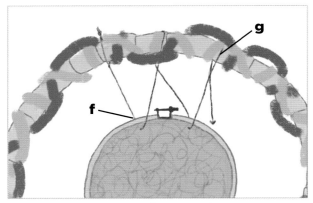

3 Mount a piece of lace fabric or a doily onto an embroidery hoop. If necessary, add a bit of glue to tack the fabric down to the backside. Trim away excess fabric (e).

4 Tie one end of the 6' (182.88cm) piece of cotton yarn to the Hula-Hoop. Thread it into a space in the edge of the mounted lace (f), and then loop the yarn back to the Hula-Hoop (g). Continue threading the embroidery hoop to the Hula-Hoop, all the while keeping the small hoop centered. Once back to the beginning, tie off the yarn and trim away excess.

TIP: Add a piece of tape to the end of the cotton string for threading the doily to the Hula-Hoop. It will form a sort of needle.

5 To embellish the dream catcher, tie extra ribbon to the bottom of the Hula-Hoop (h). Braid several pieces to add visual weight and texture. Faux-feathers can be used to add more interest (see page 14). Slits can be cut into the ends of some ribbons to be knotted to the dream catcher with a lark's head knot (i).

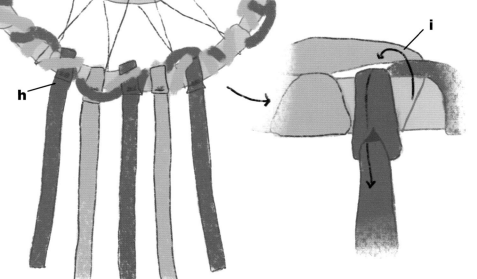

Knotty Owls

This owl pattern is quite simple because it only requires the use of a few knots. Working with fabric lends an interesting challenge: fray happens, but if this shabby-chic look is undesired, the use of ribbons will work just as well.

KNOTTY LEVEL: 1
WORKING TIME: 2 hours
FINISHED SIZE: 12" to 15" (30.48 to 38.10cm) long
CORDS: Fabric strips, ribbon, yarn
SUPPLIES

- (13) 1" x 36" (2.54 x 91.44cm) pieces of fabric
- (2) Plastic eyes (15mm)
- Oval bead or bit of cotton thread
- Optional macramé board with T-pins

DIRECTIONS

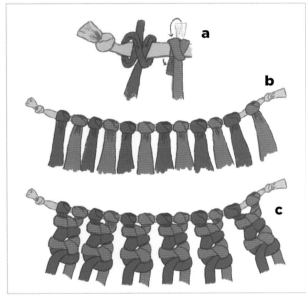

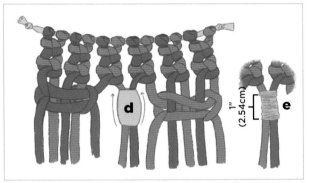

3 Find the two center strips and thread the bead (d). If a bead is not available, wrap the strands together using a piece of contrasting thread (e). The wrap should be about 1" (2.54cm) long.

1 Tie an overhand knot into the end of a fabric strip, then mount the twelve remaining strands onto the same strip using clove hitches (a). Tie another overhand knot into the original strip and trim away the excess fabric (b). Save the remaining trimming for later.

2 Tie four alternating half-hitches across the whole row (c).

FABRIC CUTTING TIP: Fold the fabric so that fabric shears can be used to make just a couple snips to form 2" (5.08cm)–wide ribbons. The fabric will fray with excess knotting. To avoid the "fray" look, use ⅝" to 1" (1.59 to 2.54cm) ribbon as an alternative.

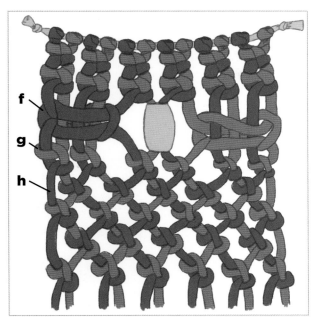

7 Take the remaining scrap piece of fabric and cut it in half. Mount the first six strands to the scrap using clove hitches (i). Cinch the knots close together, then wrap the fabric around the gathered hanging strands, tying it off with a square knot on the back side of the leg (j). Repeat with the second leg.

8 Trim the hanging strands so that they hang about 3" (7.62cm) long.

9 With scrap bits of fabric, cut three squares for each eye and snip a hole in the center (k). Mount the eyes to the owl (l).

4 Tie one large, loose square knot on either side of the bead using the first and fifth strands (f). This is to simulate the owl's eyes.

5 Form a row of two alternating half-hitches (g). On the next row, drop the first and last strands and form another row of alternate half-hitches (h).

6 Repeat step 5, forming three more rows.

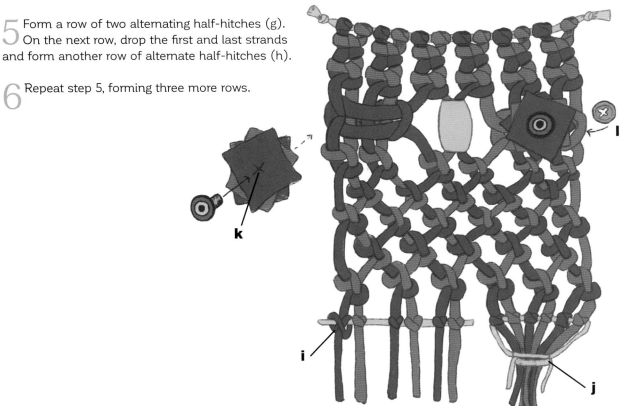

Layered Birch Hanging

This hanging was designed to imitate the look of birch wood. The dowel used is made from manufactured birch limb, which can be found in craft stores. If possible, found branches can be substituted to pay homage to nature. For a less rustic look, swap out the fabric strips for ribbon.

KNOTTY LEVEL: 1–2
WORKING TIME: 4–6 hours
FINISHED SIZE: 18" wide x 2' long (45.72 x 60.96cm)
CORDS: Jute string or twine, fabric strips or ribbon
SUPPLIES

- (12) 1" x 5' (2.54 x 152.40cm) lengths of fabric (or ribbon)
- (2) 1" x 12' (2.54 x 365.76cm) lengths of fabric
- (1) 2' (60.96cm) length of fabric or jute (for hanging)
- (10) 5' (152.40cm) lengths of jute (assorted colors)
- (4) 6' (182.88cm) lengths of jute (assorted colors)
- (1) 18" (45.72cm) branch (or a dowel rod)

DIRECTIONS

1 Tie the 2' (60.96cm) length of fabric (or jute) to both ends of the branch for hanging.

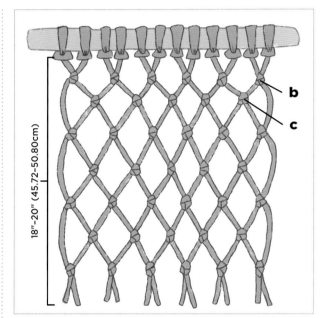

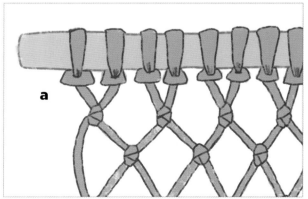

2 Cut small holes into one end of the fabric strips and tie a lark's head knots with the 5' (152.4cm)– length strips to the branch (a).

3 Tie the strands with alternating half-hitches across the row (b). On the next row, drop the first and last strands on the row. Tie alternating half-hitch knots to each of the strands to begin the formation of the net (c). The knots should settle about 1" (2.54cm) apart from the previous row.

4 Repeat step 3 until the piece measures 18" to 20" (45.72 to 50.80cm), or until there's no more fabric.

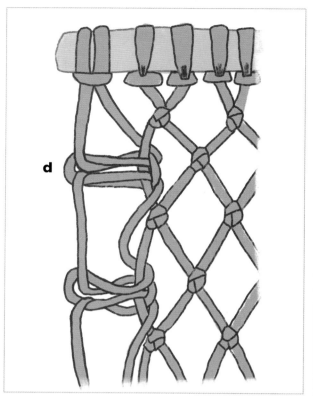

7 Form Josephine knots in the net pattern, settling each finished knot in the open space of the fabric netting (f).

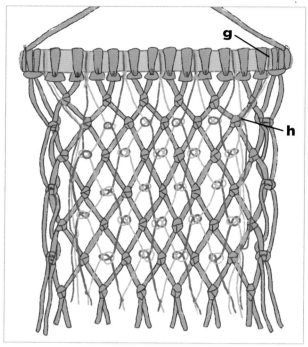

5 Tie lark's head knots to the 12' (3.66m) lengths of fabric on either end of the netting. Square knot these strands to the center of every other net opening (d). This will help straighten out the net.

8 Tie and mount the 6' (182.88cm) strands on either end of the jute net with lark's head knots (g). Tie square knots into the center of each net opening to help straighten the edge (h).

9 Trim the bottom fringe as desired and hang.

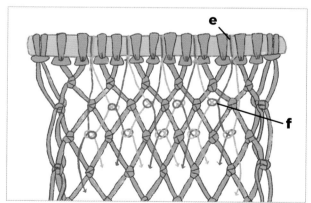

6 Tie together the mismatched colors of the jute using overhand knots, then tie them to the branch with a series of lark's head knots, mounting each piece between the first pairs of fabric (e).

Mini Sweater Hanger

This simple little hanging is designed to test knot-tying skills. Make this in a 4 to 6mm bulky cord for a larger size, or use cotton crochet yarn for a smaller design. You can also add ribbon for a shabby-chic design.

KNOTTY LEVEL: 1–2
WORKING TIME: 2 hours
FINISHED SIZE: 10" wide x 12" long (25.40 x 30.48cm)
CORDS: Cotton rope, polypropylene, cotton string or yarn, ribbon
SUPPLIES

- (1) 24" (60.96cm) strand of cotton rope (4mm)
- (4) 3' (91.44cm) lengths of cotton rope (color A)
- (4) 3' (91.44cm) lengths of cotton rope (color B)

DIRECTIONS

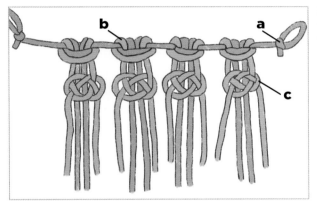

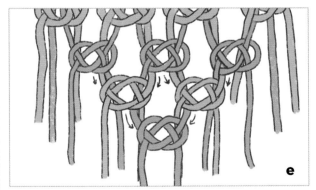

1 Tie loops into the ends of the 24" (60.96cm) length of cord so that it can be used as a hanging (a). Tie double lark's head knots with each of the 3' (91.44cm) lengths of cord onto the hanging strand (b). Color B will nest in the middle of color A.

2 Form a row of Josephine knots (or square knots) with the strands of color A (c). There will be four knots across this row.

3 For row 2, pull color B to the front, skip the first strand, form a row of three Josephine knots (or square knots), and skip the last strand (d). Repeat this decreasing method for two more rows (e).

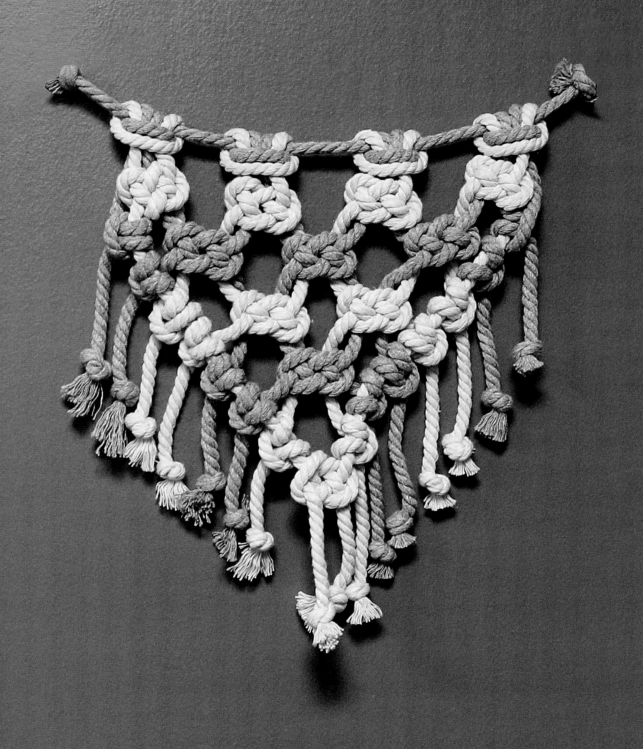

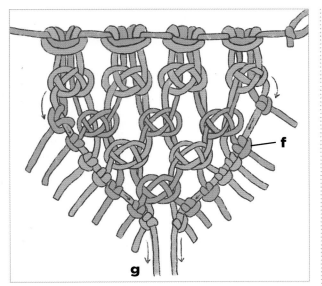

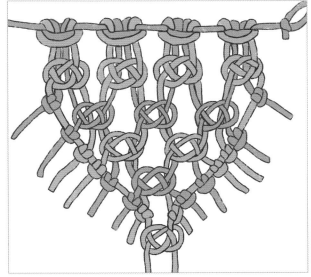

4 Draw the outside strands toward the center and clove hitch each hanging strand to these anchor cords (f). Form a Josephine knot with the two anchor cords where they meet in the middle (g).

5 Tie an overhand knot into the end of each hanging strand, about 4" (10.16cm) from the hanging. Trim away excess cord.

Variation: Use fabric strips instead of cotton rope.

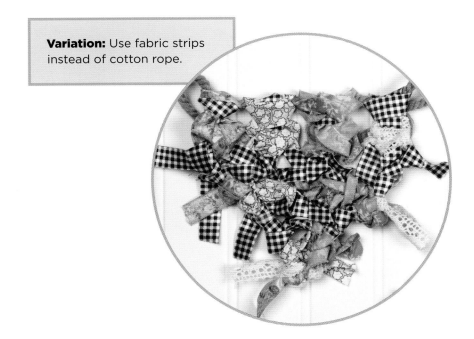

Owlet Garland

These little owls would be adorable perched over a party setting, but ideally treasured nightly above the bed or across a window. A complete string contains ten finished owlets.

KNOTTY LEVEL: 2
WORKING TIME: 4 hours
FINISHED SIZE: 11' wide x 6" tall (335.28 x 15.24cm)
CORDS: Yarns, braided or twisted cotton string or twine, ribbon or fabric strips, lightweight polypropylene or parachute cord (worsted or medium weight recommended, but this project will work on any scale)
SUPPLIES

- (3) 12' (3.66m) strands of cotton yarn (assorted colors)
- (60) 2' (60.96cm) strands of cotton yarn (assorted colors—each owl requires 12' [3.66m] total)
- (2) Puff fabric paints
- Macramé board with T-pins (optional)

DIRECTIONS

1 Start by braiding together the three 12' (3.66m) strands of yarn. Tie the three pieces together at one end with an overhand knot, braid, and finish with an overhand knot. The resulting cord will be about 11' (3.35m) long. If this task is too overwhelming, the cords can be left loose.

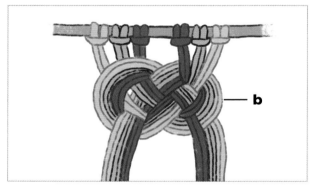

3 Tie a Josephine knot using all the cords as they are arranged (b).

TIP: Try to keep the cords flat, following the curves as the cords are arranged so that the knot doesn't tighten too much.

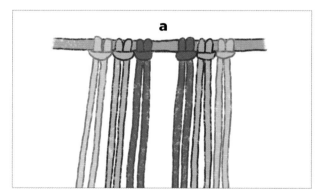

2 Mount six strands of cord to the long string using lark's head knots. Arrange so there is roughly a 1" (2.54cm) gap between the first three and second three sets (a).

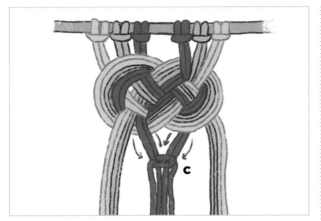

4 Gather the four centermost strands. Settle two in the center and tie one square knot with the outer strands (c).

6 Repeat the process for making owls (steps 2 to 5) until there are ten owls evenly spaced across the garland. Finish by adding a dab of puff paint to the Josephine knots (f). Allow the eyes to dry as directed.

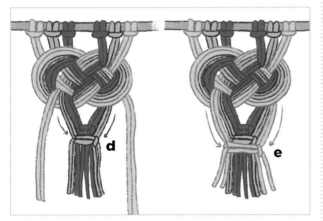

5 Find the next four inner strands, settle the two inside strands butt against the first knot, and tie another square knot around the whole grouping with the outer strands (d). Repeat with the last four strands (e). Trim the tail as desired.

Index

Resources

CONSUMER CRAFTS
www.consumercrafts.com

CREATIVITY PORTAL
www.creativity-portal.com

DICK BLICK ART MATERIALS
www.dickblick.com

FAB-U-LOOP
www.fabuloopyarn.com

HITCH & ARROW
www.hitchandarrow.com

MODERN MACRAMÉ
www.modernmacrame.com

NIROMA STUDIO
www.niromastudio.com

PEPPERELL BRAIDING COMPANY
www.pepperell.com

About the Author

© Daniel Mathieu

Samantha Grenier is a color engineer (illustrator) and macramé artist from New Hampshire. She integrates texture, simple shapes, and kisses of color to design visual impact. Macramé knotted its way into her heart during her decade-long career as a Graphic Designer in the craft industry. She finds inspiration for her art and designs by wandering through museums and nature. Her favorite sources include seashells, root vegetables, leaves, and fashion. *Macrame for Home Décor* is her third "knotty" title.

You can find her on Facebook, Twitter, YouTube, and Instagram (*@illustratorsam*) or on her website, *www.Illustrator-Sam.com.*